WASHINGTON ON THE BRAZOS

WASHINGTON ON THE BRAZOS

Cradle of the Texas Republic

BY RICHARD B. MCCASLIN

Austin
Texas State Historical Association

Library of Congress Cataloging-in-Publication Data

Names: McCaslin, Richard B., author
Title: Washington on the Brazos : cradle of the Texas Republic / by Richard
    B. McCaslin.
Other titles: Fred Rider Cotten popular history series ; no. 24.
Description: Austin : Texas State Historical Association, [2016] | Series:
    Number 24 in Fred Rider Cotten popular history series | Includes
    bibliographical references.
Identifiers: LCCN 2015042119 | ISBN 9781625110367
Subjects: LCSH: Washington (Tex.)—History. | Washington-on-the-Brazos State
    Historic Site (Tex.)—History. | Texas—History—To 1846.
Classification: LCC F394.W22 M35 2016 | DDC 976.4/245—dc23 LC record
    available at http://lccn.loc.gov/2015042119

CONTENTS

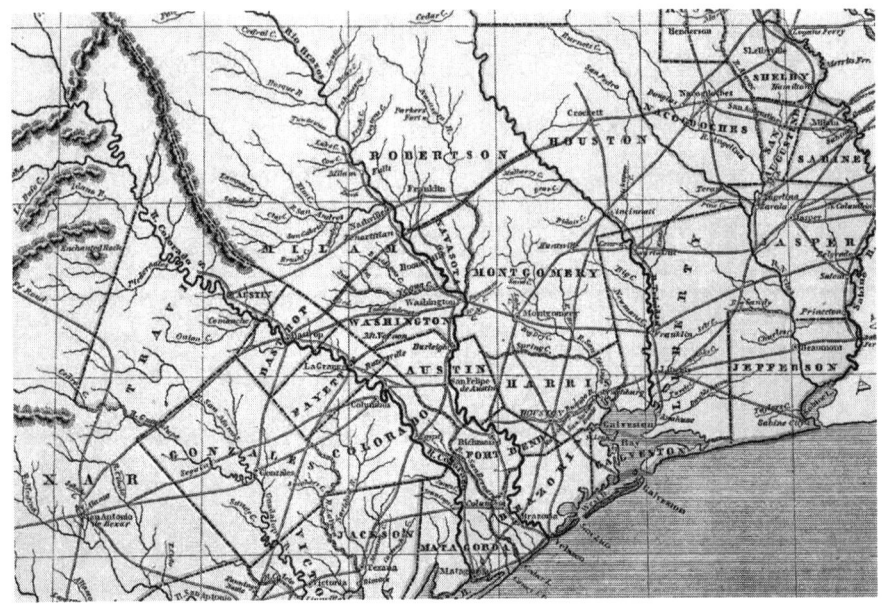

Detail showing Washington County (center) and surrounding portion of Southeast Texas. From Sidney E. Morse, *Texas* (New York: Sidney E. Morse and Samuel Breese, 1844). *UT Arlington Library Special Collections.*

PREFACE

When most people think about Washington-on-the-Brazos, they see a small white frame building close to the Brazos River. That is Independence Hall, where the Texas Declaration of Independence was signed in March 1836. What is missing from most imaginations, and indeed from the present landscape, are the many other buildings that composed the town of Washington then and later. They are as invisible as most of the story of Washington, both before and after the birth of the Republic of Texas. Created like so many Texas towns as a business venture, Washington served as a national capital twice, but it also became a county seat and venue for statewide political conventions. Male residents fought in every war, and many smaller conflicts, that involved Texas, while the ladies of the community were especially involved in supporting the embattled Confederacy. Texans love to talk about steamboats and railroads, and both had a great impact on Washington. Reconstruction looms large in the history of Washington. During the twentieth century, when many small Texas towns faded from the map, Old Washington, as it had become known, did likewise. But fortunately for the town's legacy, the site became a state park, or historic site, and Washington-on-the-Brazos continues to play a vital role in preserving the memory of the Republic of Texas.

This brief study proceeds chronologically, for the most part, through the history of the community, town, and park presently known as Washington-on-the Brazos. The first chapter focuses on the period before the Convention of 1836 established the Republic of Texas. The second discusses the events of the Republic period, while the third provides an overview of Washington's commercial boom period, from 1845 to 1855. What follows is a study of how the conflicts of the Civil War era combined with short-sighted business decisions to bring an end to prosperity. The fifth chapter provides some insights into how the struggle to define the future of Texas during and immediately after Reconstruction further undermined Washington, leaving a community that was virtually a shadow of the antebellum town. Finally, the last chapter provides a narrative of how Washington's memory became enshrined through the development of Washington-on-the-Brazos State Historic Site.

Dianne Powell, native Texan and past president of the Texas State Historical Association, suggested that the time had come for a book to be written about Washington-on-the-Brazos. Dr. Randolph B. Campbell, chief historian of the Texas State Historical Association, was kind enough to believe that I could write such a book. I thank both of them for being such insightful and trusting sponsors. Shawn Carlson, the curator of collections and exhibits for the Star of the Republic Museum at Washington-on-the-Brazos State Historic Site, is a very capable and patient scholar, and I thank her profusely for her kind assistance. Houston McGaugh, director of the Star of the Republic Museum, also answered my many questions in a patient and efficient manner. Again, thank you.

As with all of my projects, this could not have come to a successful conclusion without the support of my wife, Jana McCaslin. We have now spent two-thirds of our lives together, and I look forward to many more years to come.

Richard B. McCaslin
University of North Texas

Chapter 1

PRELUDE

Washington-on-the-Brazos State Historic Site lies just below the junction of the Brazos and Navasota Rivers in modern-day Washington County. It occupies much of the former location of the town of Washington, which lies adjacent to the small crossroads community that still bears the name. While Washington is best known as the place where the Republic of Texas began, it has a significant history that begins much earlier. Indians as well as European explorers and missionaries traveled through the region or even settled nearby. Lured to the area by the rich Blackland Prairie soil, especially in the bottoms along the Brazos, and generous changes in Spanish and Mexican land policies, Anglo homesteaders pushed the Indians aside. Beginning in the 1820s, they worked quickly to develop farms, establish a ferry where the La Bahía Road crossed the Brazos, and build a town on the bluffs overlooking the river crossing. All of this provides a substantial prelude to the better-known political events of the 1830s.

Indians were of course the first people to settle near Washington, but they were not the only ones there before Anglo settlers came. Historical records indicate that Tonkawas and Caddos lived in the area, with Apaches, Comanches, and others coming through it. French explorer René Robert Cavelier, Sieur de La Salle, arrived in 1685, but he was killed before he established permanent settlements. The Spanish responded to the French intrusion by building missions in East Texas. They blazed a road that crossed the Brazos River at the future site of Washington to link those missions to the presidio and mission at La Bahía, but they did not build anything at the river crossing. Another intruder arrived in 1819. Randall Jones, a Georgia-born veteran of the War of 1812, established a store at

Nacogdoches about 1816. Three years later he joined James Long for his filibuster into Spanish Texas and was ordered to Galveston to recruit Jean Lafitte, whom Jones had met earlier. Jones led a small force down the La Bahía Road to the Brazos and began building boats, but he was attacked in October 1819 by a more numerous Mexican detachment commanded by Lt. Col. Juan Ignacio Pérez, a veteran of the Battle of Medina in 1813 against the Gutiérrez-Magee Expedition who once served as governor of the province of Texas. Pérez later captured Long, but Jones escaped with his men and withdrew to Louisiana. Jones returned to Texas in 1822 but did not live at Washington. Ironically, many settlers there, as well as some early historians, gave the credit for his expedition to Washington County resident James Walker Sr., who did not come to Texas until 1824.[1]

Indians did not apparently become involved in the quarrels of the first white intruders in the Washington area, but conflicts erupted when Anglos began settling there. The first Anglo settler, Andrew Robinson, arrived in late 1821 as one of Stephen F. Austin's first colonists. His military experience in the Gutiérrez-Magee Expedition, which failed to win Texas independence from Spain in 1812–1813, led to his appointment as a militia captain, and he led at least one campaign against Karankawas. During the summer of 1835 a series of Caddo attacks and white reprisals prompted a small company from the Washington area to take the field under the command of William Oldham. They attacked a Caddo village, killing two Indians and burning the settlement. During their march home, one volunteer was killed and another wounded in a confused nighttime scramble in camp. Lydia Ann McHenry, who became a popular teacher, wrote to her brother that Oldham's company and other white volunteers had "done just enough to inflame the Indians & no frontier is safe."[2] Both Indians and whites continued to clash with each other in the Washington area for several more decades before Anglo settlers pushed further west.

Conflicts with Indians were not the only challenges faced by Anglo colonists such as Andrew Robinson. He probably settled at the junction of the Brazos and Navasota Rivers, on the south bank of the former, because it was the point where the La Bahía Road crossed the Brazos. The settlement of Nacogdoches had developed at the northern end of this trail, originally blazed to connect the

Placido, Chief of the Tonkawas. From Homer S. Thrall, *A Pictorial History of Texas* (St. Louis: N. D. Thompson & Company, 1879).

Caddo Chief. From Homer S. Thrall, A Pictorial History of Texas (St. Louis: N. D. Thompson & Company, 1879).

Spanish missions of East Texas with the presidio and mission at La Bahía. This meant that travelers, with money and trade goods, would be coming his way. Either when he arrived or shortly afterward, Robinson began operating a ferry at the river crossing, supplementing his farm production with the fees he collected. A small advertisement in the *Texas State Gazette* on October 9, 1830, revealed that Robinson also operated a "house of Entertainment within a few yards of said Ferry, where travelers, and others with their horses, may be comfortably accommodated." Having received two leagues and a labor of land, or just over nine thousand acres, as one of the Old Three Hundred, Austin's original colonists, Robinson was well settled on the Brazos by the early 1830s.[3]

Robinson, born in 1770, was not a young man when he arrived on the Brazos, and so he welcomed a partner soon after his arrival. His son-in-law, John W. Hall, who was also a veteran of the Gutiérrez-Magee Expedition, settled nearby and joined him in farming and operating the ferry. Hall apparently had greater ambitions than his father-in-law, and Robinson provided him with the opportunity to expand his economic interests. Hall did not need more land or laborers. He received two leagues and two labors in 1824 as one of Austin's Old Three Hundred, as well as another league in 1830. Furthermore, a census in 1826 noted that he owned twenty slaves. But Hall's property was located elsewhere, while Robinson began giving him the land along the Brazos near the ferry crossing. Robinson gave 640 acres to Hall and his wife, Patsy Robinson Hall, in May 1831, in return for their promise to care for him in his old age. During April 1835 Robinson sold the remainder of his Brazos tract to Hall. A month earlier, Hall had organized the Washington Townsite Association with Asa Hoxey, Thomas Gray, and partners James B. Miller and Alexander Somervell as co-investors. Others later claimed that Robert M. Williams, who lived downriver at San Felipe, chose the name for the new community, but it is more likely that Hoxey chose the name in honor of his hometown in Georgia. Each investor (Miller and Somervell counted as one) received 160 acres from the land given to Hall by Robinson in 1831; in turn, they gave Hall $1,800. He also retained control of the ferry and three town lots to be surveyed, and he served as agent for all other lot sales, from which the proceeds were divided equally.[4]

Horatio Chriesman, the official surveyor for Austin's Colony

Asa Hoxey. *Courtesy of Star of the Republic Museum, Blinn College, Washington-on-the-Brazos State Historic Site, Washington, Texas.*

who had originally located Robinson's property, platted the new town in the spring of 1835. Laid out in a customary grid on the bluffs along the Brazos River bank to the south and west of the ferry, Washington had ninety-two square blocks that measured three hundred feet on each side. Inside each block were twelve lots, each fifty feet wide and one hundred and fifty feet long. Thirty-five lots sold in 1835, allegedly for more than enough money to reimburse the original investors; then auctions were held in January and March 1836, January 1837, and March 1838. An additional twenty-nine lots were sold in 1836 outside of the auctions. When Hall left Washington in 1840, Joseph H. Wood succeeded him as the sales agent for the community. Wood, who had previously purchased ten lots in Washington, received another three hundred acres for his services. While there were later legal conflicts over titles, Hall's idea to plat a town on his property proved to be a financial success for him and his partners.[5]

The new community quickly became the seat of a new municipality in the Mexican province of Texas. A request had been forwarded in 1834 after a decree by the legislature of Coahuila y Tejas in March 1834 provided for the organization of municipalities within the new Department of the Brazos, but it had not arrived in time to be acted upon. In July 1835, seventy men signed a petition to James B. Miller, the political chief of the Department of the Brazos, asking again to establish a municipality. Miller, who clearly had a strong interest as an investor, approved the request, seven polling places including the town of Washington were established, and elections were held to complete the organization. Among the newly elected officers was John W. Hall, who within a year was serving as judge of the district. Others included Joshua Hadley as *alcalde*, Asa Mitchell and Jesse Grimes as *regidores*, and A. C. Reynolds as *síndico procurador*.[6]

With lots being sold and a government in place, it was not long before a community began to grow on Robinson's old homestead. Early development of course centered on Ferry Street, which led down to the landing. Buildings began at Water Street, where the land rose to a level high enough to protect most edifices from the periodic flooding of the Brazos River. This was a very serious concern. When William Fairfax Gray came to Washington in early 1836, he noticed marshy land on either side of the Brazos, with marks on the trees showing that floods had risen twenty to thirty feet above the riverbanks. John W. Lockhart, who as a child came with his parents to settle in Washington in 1839, recalled the flood-water marks on the trees as well. He also remembered that travelers on the ferry could not see the town. People had to walk up two rises, or bluffs, before they would see houses and buildings. Gray,

Lockhart, and others noted also that the townsite itself was cluttered with tree stumps; the community sat in a post oak grove, and residents used the handy timber for construction.[7]

High water on the Brazos River could be troublesome for anyone building homes and shops in Washington, but it also provided the means for prosperity. The town lay at the effective head of navigation on the Brazos. Hidalgo Falls about six miles upriver blocked water travel except in very high water. Below that, captains could bring shallow draft vessels up from the Gulf of Mexico. Early trade on the Brazos usually traveled by fairly primitive means. When the river rose, enterprising individuals built flatboats for a one-way trip downriver to the Gulf. This could be especially profitable if their cargo was cotton. For traveling upriver, though, flatboats were almost useless. Basil M. Hatfield and a partner as early as 1838 advertised for investors to finance building a keelboat, and thirteen years later P. Cleveland and his brothers launched a keelboat, the *Texas Ranger*, that carried goods as far upriver as Washington and even beyond. Again, however, this was hard work, and not always reliable. Investors needed something more dependable, and the arrival of the *Cayuga* in 1834 demonstrated that the future lay in steamboats. The owner of the *Cayuga* was William P. Harris of New York. He had his side-wheeler built at Pittsburgh, named it for his hometown, and brought it to Texas, attracted to the Brazos River by promises of land from cotton farmers. A Houston newspaper claimed that Harris was stranded by falling water levels and planted three corn crops before the river rose enough to allow him to return downstream. This tale was presented by Texans anxious after World War II to build four dams on the Brazos for water management. They had to prove the river was not navigable, and so they did. Whether or not it was true, Harris sold his steamboat to the Republic government during the Texas Revolution. Refitted with cannons as the *Branch T. Archer*, it was sent to defend Galveston and did not return to the Brazos.[8]

Washington within a year of its establishment had about one hundred people, with fifty homes and other buildings. The latter included two hotels operated by John A. Lott and Stephen R. Roberts, each of whom also had a saloon in their establishment, and a boardinghouse owned by Pamelia D. Mann, who later became wealthier and more notorious as the proprietor of a hotel in Houston. Samuel Heath had a carpenter shop, Noah T. Byars had a blacksmith shop, and there was at least one grocery store, tended by Moses T. Martin and Robert J. Clow. Dr. Benjamin B. Goodrich bought a lot in Washington in December 1835, and Dr. Richard R. Peebles joined him in January 1836. Lydia Ann McHenry, in her July 1835 letter that harshly criticized the Anglo volunteers sent to chastise the Indians, provided a hard-eyed perspective on the community: "The town is improving & will soon be as good as the other towns in the country, that is a few houses, stores, grog-shops, taverns & a billiard room. But there will be money circulating there." Mary Austin Holley, cousin of *empresario* Stephen F. Austin, wanted to encourage immigration, so she was more kind: "It is quite a new town, but is increasing very rapidly, and already numbers fifty houses." Warming to her subject, she added, "It is pleasantly and healthfully situated; and, with the numerous advantages which it enjoys, cannot fail to become an important point in Texas."[9]

War with the Mexican government of Gen. Antonio López de Santa Anna brought new faces to town. Santa Anna was not sympathetic to demands for self-government from outlying states and provinces, and by the mid-1830s Texans and others were rebelling against his highly centralized regime. Austin traveled to Mexico City to meet with Santa Anna but was arrested and held for more than a year because of an incendiary letter he wrote to the *ayuntamiento* in San Antonio. Released, he returned to Texas in the late summer of 1835 to find that even more of his colonists were in a rebellious mood. Many of them had not yet decided if they wanted statehood and a restoration of the Constitution of 1824 or independence and their own plan of government, but they opposed Santa Anna. Washington blacksmith Noah T. Byars even wrote a defiant poem calling on fellow Texans to oppose the "martial law" of Santa Anna. That same summer, former legislator Mirabeau B. Lamar of Georgia, who was in the area to claim a headright, attended a meeting at Washington and made a speech in which he declared that if fighting began, he would share the fate of Texas "for good or ill." Lamar did not reveal his low opinion of his new acquaintances' political intellect to them, which was probably just as well, considering his later political ambitions.[10]

When war erupted in the fall of 1835, Washington settlers joined

Noah T. Byars. *Courtesy of Star of the Republic Museum, Blinn College, Washington-on-the-Brazos State Historic Site, Washington, Texas.*

in the conflict. Andrew Robinson allegedly fought under the "Come and Take It" banner at Gonzales in October, when Texans repulsed an effort by San Antonio garrison troops to reclaim a cannon. James G. Swisher led a company from Washington that arrived too late to fight at Gonzales, but his men, among whom was surveyor Horatio Chriesman, did fight in the siege and capture of San Antonio in December. Swisher was one of three commissioners appointed to receive the surrender of Gen. Martín Perfecto de Cos. He later led most of his troops home, but not all of them. William R. Carey had arrived at Washington in late July 1835, intending to settle there, but in October the news of the impending clash at Gonzales lured him to the fight. He quickly became a lieutenant of artillery and was slightly wounded while working his gun close to enemy barricades in the streets of San Antonio during the December attack. Elected captain of a company, he stayed at San Antonio and took charge of the guns in the Alamo.[11]

Volunteers streamed into Washington during late 1835 and early 1836. Among the many newcomers were a detachment of the New Orleans Greys and David Crockett with his company of Tennessee volunteers. Byars repaired several weapons for the Greys during November 1835, before they departed for the attack on San Antonio, and then worked for other would-be soldiers as well. Crockett and several of his men stayed at the hotel owned by John A. Lott, who within a few months would be the agent of a new government at Washington, sending volunteers to their assigned posts. Some of course did not wait for instructions: Asa Walker borrowed a coat and gun from his friend William W. Gant, with whom he had come to Texas in late 1835, left a note of apology, and hurried to join the garrison at the Alamo. The visitors were not always impressed with Washington, or Lott. One New Orleans Grey, Herman Ehrenberg, kindly wrote: "The little town on the edge of these sylvan depths had already a thriving and prosperous look." William P. Zuber was less impressed, recalling that there were only three good frame houses, one of which was Lott's establishment; the rest were "a few pole cabins." William Fairfax Gray was most unkind. To him, Lott's operation was "a wretchedly made establishment" with "a blackguard, rowdy set lounging about." As for the town itself, "It is laid out in the woods; about a dozen wretched cabins or shanties constitute the city; not one decent house in it, and only one well defined street, which consists of an opening cut out of the woods." He added that he was "glad to get out of so disgusting a place."[12]

While Texans fought and won several clashes, the political debate continued over the future of Texas. Two councils had already been held; the second had sent Austin to speak with Santa Anna. When plans were laid in the late summer of 1835 for a third meeting, to be called a consultation to dispel suspicions about the delegate's intentions, a split immediately developed over whether it would meet at San Felipe de Austin or Washington on October 15, 1835. When that day came, a large number of delegates were in San Felipe, but a smaller number assembled in Washington, including the delegates from that municipality: Phillip H. Coe, Elijah Collard, Jesse Grimes, Asa Hoxey, and Asa Mitchell. There not being a quorum in either place, it was decided to attempt to assemble again in San Felipe on November 1. Despite a decree from the Permanent Council, organized by Austin, that the meeting should take place in Washington, more delegates stubbornly assembled at San Felipe during the first days of November 1835, and the few who gathered in Washington reluctantly agreed to join them.[13]

The consultation at San Felipe created a provisional state government for Texas, with a General Council, Henry Smith as governor, and Sam Houston as general-in-chief. Provisions were then discussed for a convention to establish a more permanent government, including the question of where this gathering would occur. When Houston introduced a resolution to meet in Washington, primarily because it was a more central location, concerns resurfaced about its lack of public facilities and a newspaper with a press to print official documents. Many delegates probably agreed with Gray that Washington was a "rare place to hold a national convention in" and that they might "have to leave it promptly to avoid starvation." When the General Council narrowly approved Houston's proposal, Smith vetoed it. Foreshadowing the political conflict to come, the Council approved a second measure to meet at Washington, adding the date of March 1, 1836, and then overrode Smith's subsequent, second veto. On February 22, 1836, after declaring Smith removed as governor, the Council moved to Washington, where the convention met on March 1 as provided. One of the first orders of business was to abolish the provisional state government, and on March 11 the Council met for the last time.[14]

What may have convinced the General Council to move to Washington was the offer of a building in which the impending convention could meet free of charge. Noah T. Byars and Peter M. Mercer had an unfinished frame building at the corner of Ferry and Main Streets, which they had apparently built with the hope that someone would rent it. Eleven local businessmen agreed to pay $170 for the use of the building for three months: land agent and ferryman

Sam Houston. *Library of Congress Prints & Photographs Division, Washington, D. C.*

John W. Hall, hotel operators John A. Lott and Stephen R. Roberts, merchants Moses T. Martin and Robert J. Clow, Dr. Richard R. Peebles, Dr. William P. Smith (also a Methodist Protestant minister who had served as a surgeon for Austin's troops in the fall of 1835), land agent Joseph H. Wood, John G. Caldwell, John C. Neal, and

G. P. Patrick. Descriptions of the facility vary, but most who visited it agreed that it was far from impressive. The ever-critical Gray wrote that it was an "unfinished house, without doors or windows. In lieu of glass, cotton cloth was stretched across the windows, which partially excluded the cold wind." Another visitor recalled a "bad painting on canvas" that hung in one window, depicting an eagle "smashing to pieces" the "edifice of centralism in Mexico" with "spears and Jupiter's lightning bolts." Even worse than that, at least for Byars and Mercer, was that the convention abruptly adjourned after using the building for less than three weeks, so the local boosters, as well as the Republic and state of Texas, never paid them.[15]

By the time that the General Council settled in Washington, Houston has already been there and gone. He was ordered by Smith on December 2, 1835, to establish his headquarters in the new community and arrived on Christmas Day, but he issued a decree calling for "Citizens of Texas" to rally against Mexico on December 12 that had Washington as his "Head Quarters" in the letterhead. Houston apparently did not like Washington; there was no public celebration of New Year's Day, and on January 2 he wrote to an associate that he was "most miserably cool & sober." Disgusted with the conflict between Smith and the Council, Houston left Washington to visit with Indians in East Texas, ostensibly to secure their promise that they would not support Santa Anna. He would return soon, however, and the new community on the bluffs overlooking the Brazos River would provide a stage for events that were far more dramatic than anything that had previously occurred on Andrew Robinson's old homestead.[16]

Chapter 2
POLITICAL SEAT

Washington may be best known as the birthplace of the Republic of Texas, but the town served twice more as the seat of Texas government before statehood. The delegates to the Convention of 1836 left hastily in mid-March, but Republic leaders returned during the fall of 1842, and the Texas Congress made its last decisions, including annexation, in Washington during 1845. The town also became the seat of Washington County. Meanwhile, Washington residents fought Indians and Mexicans while trying at the same time to establish the customary social institutions, such as schools and churches, in their community. The problem was always a lack of money, as it would not be until after statehood that Washington enjoyed its greatest period of commercial success.

Washington in 1836 did not offer the Convention delegates much except a free meeting place and a central location. They and other visitors had to scramble for official and personal space. As perhaps they expected when they offered a building for the Convention, Washington hotel owners John A. Lott and Stephen R. Roberts enjoyed a booming business. Other residents offered far less desirable facilities to desperate lodgers. Samuel Heath rented his carpenter shop to San Antonio delegates Jesse B. Badgett, José Antonio Navarro, and José Francisco Ruiz, as well as Lorenzo de Zavala of Harrisburg and William Fairfax Gray. The latter, who attended the Convention only as an observer, insisted that Heath install a floor before he signed the lease. The sparse building provided little more than a place for the delegates to sleep. Gray ate his meals at Pamelia D. Mann's boardinghouse, where of course the fare did not meet his expectations.[17]

The Convention quickly disposed of important business under

the direction of President Richard Ellis, who had previously attended the Constitutional Convention of Alabama in 1818. A committee led by George C. Childress produced a Declaration of Independence, which was adopted on March 2, 1836 (Sam Houston's forty-third birthday). When the delegates began signing it the next day, George W. Barnett, Benjamin B. Goodrich, Jesse Grimes, and James G. Swisher endorsed it for the municipality of Washington. On March 5, Houston was confirmed as overall commander of the Texan armies, and on March 6 he departed for Gonzales, where he joined his troops in the field. The assembly also began discussing at length the terms of a constitution for the new republic.[18]

The fall of the Alamo to Gen. Antonio López de Santa Anna, with the loss of its entire garrison, galvanized the Convention into working more quickly. Letters from Houston and Juan Seguín on March 15, 1836, reported the debacle, but the news was doubted until the arrival of John Sutherland from Gonzales on March 16 with an eyewitness confirmation. The constitution was hurriedly finished by midnight, and then the delegates spent another four hours electing and installing the officers of the interim government of the Republic. David G. Burnet, who came to Washington to file an appeal for his two clients in a capital murder case, was inaugurated as the president of the Republic of Texas at two in the morning on March 17. He became the default choice for the Texans since Stephen F. Austin was seeking aid in the United States with William H. Wharton, who had presided over a previous council, and Houston was with the army. Zavala became the new vice president.[19]

Burnet may have just been in the right place at the right time to become interim president of the Republic of Texas, but he did provide strong leadership. Having completed their work, most of the delegates joined in the "general panic," as Gray described it. S. F. Sparks recalled that the news of the fall of Alamo "spread like wild fire in high grass." Rumors surfaced within hours that Gen. José Urrea, Santa Anna's second-in-command, was approaching with thousands of cavalrymen. But Burnet stayed in Washington for three more days with his secretary of war, Thomas J. Rusk, and secretary of the navy, Robert M. Potter. Hotel owner John A. Lott kept his place open for them, but they may not have slept much as hasty preparations had to be made for an orderly military withdrawal. The Convention had declared all men ages seventeen to fifty liable

David G. Burnet. From Homer S. Thrall, *A Pictorial History of Texas* (St. Louis: N. D. Thompson & Company, 1879).

for military service, promising land grants to those who served. Henry Teal's company had guarded the delegates as they worked, while hundreds of other volunteers arrived to await instructions. Now Sparks and others were enlisted to ferry cotton bales across the Brazos River and stack them as a makeshift breastwork. Rusk posted Sparks's detachment there with orders not to let any armed man cross and to impress all the powder, lead, and horses that they could find for the army. Sparks claimed that a woman shouldered a musket and stood guard one night when her husband refused to do so.[20]

Burnet and his secretaries left town on March 20, 1836, leaving Washington almost deserted. Some men, such as James G. Swisher and Horatio Chriesman, joined Houston at Gonzales, but they and others were allowed to leave the army and escort their families east in what became known as the Runaway Scrape. Before he crossed the Brazos, Rusk issued orders for the creation of another mounted company, the Washington Guards, under the command of Capt. Joseph B. Chance, who had followed Swisher to San Antonio in the fall of 1835. Chance enlisted thirty-eight men, including Richard R. Peebles and Stephen R. Roberts, two of the men who had brought the Convention to town by providing a building. The company lingered for a brief time, but then hurried to join Houston as he retreated eastward. When he turned to crush Santa Anna at San Jacinto on April 21, 1836, the Washington Guards were nearby, guarding baggage and tending convalescents at Harrisburg.[21]

Many men in Washington continued in military service during the early years of the Republic. After the Runaway Scrape, Gen. Thomas J. Green led a mounted force through the Washington area in June 1836 to watch for Indians. A few weeks later, Texas Secretary of War Thomas J. Rusk appointed John G. W. Pierson as captain of Post Washington. Pierson enrolled sixty-seven men by the end of June. They patrolled for three months along the Brazos, and two were killed in a fight with Comanches in August 1836, before the post was deactivated and the company disbanded. During the same summer, William W. Hill mustered another Washington County company. Among his troopers were George W. Barnett and John P. Coles, both of whom later served with Hill in the Congress of the Republic of Texas.[22]

Conflicts between settlers and Indians continued to plague the Republic, with some of the most notable fights being the campaigns against the Cherokees in East Texas, in 1837–1838, and the Council House Fight at San Antonio and the subsequent Comanche raid on Linnville in 1840. Closer to Washington, a clash on Elm Creek in January 1837 again resulted in casualties among whites as well as the Indians, and alarms spread to the Brazos settlements. The next month, Joel W. Robison of Washington, who had been with William Oldham during his expedition in 1835, was visiting his father, John G. Robison, in Fayette County. The elder Robison was home from Columbia, where he served in the first Congress of the

Republic, and went with his brother Walter to deliver supplies to a friend who lived five miles away. Joel became worried, searched for the two older men, and found their corpses stripped, mutilated, and scalped, apparently by Comanches. When Caddos killed several Anglo settlers within fifteen miles of Washington in June 1837, Pierson again raised a company to patrol the area.[23]

Indians did not pose the most serious threat to Washington during its first decade of existence. Abandonment of the town during the Runaway Scrape in March 1836 interrupted its economic development, and the Panic of 1837 almost completely cancelled it. Optimistic residents gathered for a procession and an elegant dinner at Stephen R. Roberts's hotel on March 2, 1837, in honor of the first year of independence. Before they adjourned for a grand ball, the vice president of the organizing committee, Robert M. Stevenson, offered an interesting toast: "Uncle Sam's big corn field, and his son Sam's big cotton patch, may they soon be united in one great plantation." Cantankerous William Fairfax Gray visited Washington in late March and found it to be three times larger than he remembered and still growing. Such optimism proved premature, however, as neither annexation nor prosperity were immediately forthcoming. When John W. Lockhart arrived in 1839, he observed that Washington had about 250 residents and 100 nonresidents. The latter, mostly horse racers and gamblers, frequented two saloons, the largest of which was operated by Basil M. Hatfield, and a racetrack that had been built as an investment in 1838 by the Jockey Club, whose secretary was Thomas P. Shapard. Hatfield, who purchased his place in 1837, had served under Sam Houston in 1836 and named his first son for him. Shapard was an attorney and Texas army veteran who was elected clerk of the district court in 1837, the same year that he bought some town lots in Washington. With the $80 to $100 entry fees his organization charged, he was able to pay purses of $300 to $500, a strong lure for racers and gamblers. The Jockey Club races continued at least through the fall of 1845.[24]

Apart from the saloons and horse races, economic matters did not improve much for Washington in the early 1840s. Lockhart remembered that there were two hotels and three stores open when he came; by 1842 he recalled that all of these had closed. He may have been wrong about the hotel operated by Stephen R. Roberts, which continued to operate for many years in Washington, but the other hotel owner, Henry R. Cartmell, opened a leather goods shop about that time. Both men were certainly more fortunate than the previous proprietor of the Washington Hotel: Thornton W. Pinckard was shot by his brother-in-law, James S. Steele, in an "affair of honor" in April 1838 and died several months later despite the efforts of Washington physician Richard R. Peebles. Pinckard was not the only victim of violence in early Washington. Col. James R. Cook returned from the Somervell Expedition in 1842 only to be shot and killed during an argument over a horse in March 1843. As for the stores, the operation owned by Edward Bailey, Thomas Gay, and Asa Hoxey closed after Gay, a San Jacinto veteran, was killed by Comanches at the Battle of Bird's Creek in 1839. David Ayres, a Washington merchant who as a schoolmaster had received William B. Travis's final letter from the Alamo (asking Ayres to care for Travis's young son), moved west, and then settled in Galveston. E. S. Cabler may have closed his shop, as Lockhart claimed, but he stayed in Washington and later did well as a merchant. But overall Lockhart's recollection of a small town in crisis by the early 1840s was fairly accurate. Adolphus Sterne passed through Washington in 1842 and reported: "a fine Place, but all the fine Stores and dwelling Houses most all deserted."[25]

Economic hardships and rough attitudes also hindered efforts to establish churches and schools. When Texas was a Mexican province only Catholic churches were legal, so when the Reverend Henry Stephenson of the Methodist Church in 1824 delivered a sermon at the future site of Washington, it did not lead to organizing a church. The Republic of Texas did not have such restrictions, and the Missionary Society of the Methodist Episcopal Church in 1837 appointed the Reverend Martin Ruter, president of Allegheny College in Pennsylvania, as superintendent of its new mission in Texas. The Reverends Robert Alexander and Littleton Fowler were chosen to serve as his assistants and actually arrived before him. Alexander explored as far west as Washington, where he found people to be "recklessly wicked" despite the claims of a few to be Methodist or Baptist. He ignored warnings and held a church service in a room over Hatfield's saloon, impressing if not converting the gamblers whose games he had interrupted. Fowler joined Alexander and

Martin Ruter. From C. C. Cody, "Rev. Martin Ruter, A. M., D. D.," *Texas Methodist Historical Quarterly* 1 (July 1909).

conducted a church service in November 1837 at a schoolhouse in Washington.[26]

Alexander returned east, meeting with Ruter as he crossed the Sabine into Texas in the fall of 1837. Ruter traveled west through Washington and visited with David Ayres, who had earlier accompanied him on his journey to Texas, and John W. Kenney, a Methodist minister from Pennsylvania who had previously worked with Ruter. Kenney in 1833 had actually built the first cabin on the future site of Washington, but within a year he had moved further west in

Washington County, to his own homestead. More important, Kenney had convened the camp meeting, for which Ayres served as secretary, that asked the Missionary Society for support, bringing Ruter and his assistants to Texas. Fowler met with Ruter when he returned to Houston; then once again Ruter rode west, meeting with Methodists and converting others. He arrived at Washington in December 1837 with Ayres. The well-traveled superintendent then settled at the home of Joseph B. Chance, the San Jacinto veteran who had been one of the few to welcome Alexander and Fowler earlier in the year.[27]

Ruter worked hard in Washington, but his stay there proved to be tragically short. He established four circuits, one of which of course focused on Washington, and he built a church on two town lots given to Fowler. There Ruter organized a Sunday school, with a library of 150 books brought from New Orleans, and welcomed fellow ministers such as Alexander, Kenney, A. P. Manly, and William P. Smith. The latter was a Tennessee veteran of the War of 1812 who, after serving with Stephen F. Austin's troops, had been appointed post surgeon at Washington by Sam Houston in December 1835, served at San Jacinto, and later became a regimental surgeon in the army of the Republic of Texas. Ruter left for his home in Pennsylvania in April 1838, but he became ill and returned to Washington. Despite the efforts of Manly, who was also a physician, and Smith, Ruter died at the age of fifty-four before dawn on May 16, 1838, after an illness of three weeks. He was buried that afternoon, after a "Divine Service" led by Manly. The following morning his small congregation gathered in his church to compose a resolution to be published in newspapers as a memorial to their fallen leader. Alexander later arranged for an inscribed slab of marble to be placed over his grave.[28]

After Ruter's demise, Methodists in Washington apparently relied on Alexander and Smith, who was actually a Methodist Protestant, and circuit riders such as Orceneth Fisher, who also served as a chaplain to the Texas Congress. It is interesting to note that early Methodists like Ruter and Ayres were always careful to provide services for blacks in the Washington area. Remarkably, John Mark, a slave from Independence, Texas, preached at Washington, as he did at other places in the county. He sometimes attracted more whites than blacks to his sermons and became so popular that some local planters, when his owner moved away, bought him and gave the deed for him to three Methodist ministers. Lockhart later claimed that Mark bought his freedom with money given to him by people who came to hear him speak. In 1853, the Texas Conference of the Methodist Episcopal Church South elected Mark as a deacon.[29]

A Methodist minister may have been the first to preach a sermon on the future site of Washington, but when Ruter arrived in Washington for the first time in December 1837, among those who greeted him was a Baptist minister, Zenos N. Morrell, who had already organized a church in the community. Morrell bought two town lots at Washington in November 1836, and he soon opened a shop for producing furniture and house trim on two lathes powered by horses. In early 1837 he founded the "first missionary Baptist church west of the Brazos river." His church only had eight members, among whom were Anderson Buffington, himself a Baptist minister and later a newspaper editor; Noah T. Byars, who was then serving as the sergeant-at-arms for the Texas Senate; Henry R. Cartmell; and Joseph H. Wood. Cartmell, who had been a deacon in Nashville, Tennessee, became a deacon for Morrell. The congregation initially met in a "small house," but by the time that Ruter came to town, they had already raised money by subscription and built a church.[30]

Morrell, whose nickname was allegedly "Wildcat," had been advised to move west from Tennessee to improve his health, and it must have worked. He founded several churches while also working as a land speculator, merchant, politician, and schoolteacher. He certainly did not back down from a challenge. He recalled a union meeting in 1838 at Washington that included him, Methodists Alexander and Smith, and Cumberland Presbyterians A. Roark and Alexander McGowan. The event was held in a former billiard hall and lasted for days. During the second evening, hecklers outside became quite imaginative. One tormented a chicken, causing it to make a racket, while a large black man occasionally yelled "Glory to God" through an open window, prompting others standing around him on the gallery to add their own catcalls. All of them were drunk, according to Morrell. Infuriated, Morrell struck the black man in the head with his cane on his second appearance in the window, and others sternly told the hecklers that they would use more deadly weapons if the trouble continued. The hecklers dispersed after a final warning from Mathew Caldwell, a signer of the Texas Declaration of Independence and a veteran of the Texas army who had settled briefly in Washington. The next day Caldwell chaired a town meeting at which resolutions condemning the hecklers were adopted, eliminating Morrell's problem.[31]

The Baptists in Washington built a church, obtained a house for Morrell, and planned for a school, but all activity ended in 1839 when Morrell left. When William M. Tryon visited two years later, he found no building or congregation. Tryon, a native of New York who graduated from Mercer College in Georgia, had been dispatched to Texas by the American Baptist Home Missionary Society, so he worked hard to resurrect the church in Washington. He enjoyed the support of some strong allies; once, when he could not conduct a meeting due to a family illness, Judge Robert E. B. Baylor took his place, conducted sermons for two weeks, and even baptized forty-two people in the Brazos River. Thirty of these converts joined Tryon's tiny congregation, which included two slaves. Cartmell became his deacon, which proved fortunate because Tryon was soon serving several churches in the county. He settled at Independence but remained active in Washington, including terms as a chaplain for the Texas Congress.[32]

Efforts to provide formal education began about a year after Washington was founded. Jane Ann Haralson Pinckard, the wife of the ill-fated Thornton W. Pinckard who was killed in a duel in 1838, was allegedly the first teacher in Washington, although the first school opened in 1837 under the direction of Patsy Robinson Hall, wife of John W. Hall. Hall's place, a log cabin, stood two miles outside of town. Frances J. S. Trask also taught in Washington for several years, but she soon moved further west and opened other schools. Eager to establish a more substantial institution, local leaders in June 1837 successfully petitioned the Texas Congress for a charter for Washington College. Its trustees included Methodists and Baptists: John P. Coles, Thomas Gay, Asa Hoxey, Stephen R. Roberts, William P. Smith, and Joseph H. Wood. William W. Gant, who had briefly edited the *Texas Reporter* at Washington and fought at San Jacinto, introduced the college bill as Washington

County's representative, but he did not secure a grant of five leagues of land as the trustees asked. Without this financial support, Washington College apparently failed to open.[33]

The Masons established the most enduring school in Washington prior to the Civil War. Phoenix Lodge No. 8, a Scottish Rite organization, received a charter in November 1838, less than a year after the establishment of the Grand Lodge in Texas. George Fisher represented the Phoenix Lodge at the next Grand Lodge meeting, and he served as the secretary of the state organization for the next two years. Henry R. Cartmell became Master of the Phoenix Lodge, but by about 1841 it stopped meeting, perhaps due to the economic decline of the town during that period. The return of the Republic government in 1842 revived interest in Masonry, and the Grand Lodge met at Washington during the first month of 1843, 1844, and 1845. Washington Lodge No. 18 got a charter from the Grand Lodge at its January 1844 meeting. Within a few years a York Rite organization appeared, chartered as Washington Chapter No. 5.[34]

Methodist minister Lindsay P. Rucker opened the Washington Masonic Academy in "an old shell of a house" about one mile south of Washington in the fall of 1839. Wood, Hall, and Henry R. Cartmell were among the first trustees. Rucker allowed only boys to attend, which proved ironic when he allegedly decided to leave "on account of the wildness of his pupils." He may also have been vexed by a lack of money, as again the Texas Congress did not provide a land grant. Judge William H. Ewing, who later served as editor of the Washington *Lone Star*, succeeded Rucker. Sadly for him, Ewing was very deaf, and soon gave up teaching to focus on his law practice. After Ewing came a teacher with the last name of Nash, an Alabama lawyer who had a bad temper, suffered from boils, and was allegedly bitten by a snake. By the fall of 1844 the academy was closed, but it would be revived.[35]

While the Washington Masonic Academy offered education for boys, the arrival of the four Sims sisters—Ann, Maria, Martha, and Elizabeth—along with the "old Lady," widow Louisa Swisher Lewis, provided the staff for a girls' school that opened during the fall of 1843. Academic courses were provided as well as instruction on the arts and piano lessons, which Lewis directed. A female pupil later recalled that Ann, the oldest sister, was understood to have worked as governess for the children of the governor of South

Carolina; whether this was true or not, she was an intimidating teacher. Matrimony seems to have derailed this educational effort. Lewis, despite the disapproval of Ann, married John S. "Rip" Ford, who originally came to Washington as a congressman, and moved to Austin. John M. Swisher, the son of James G. Swisher and a San Jacinto veteran who served as a clerk in the auditor's office for the Republic, the Texas Congress, and the Annexation Convention, married Maria. Swisher and his wife also followed the government to Austin, and allegedly her sisters went with them. A guide to Texas reported that Washington had an academy open in 1845, but that may have been a short-lived operation under the direction of Baptist minister Benjamin B. Baxter, who served the church in Washington but lived in Independence.[36]

The recovery of churches and schools in Washington by the mid-1840s was largely due to its becoming the capital of the Republic of Texas again. The leaders of the Republic left in a hurry in mid-March 1836, and they stayed away for more than six years. In the meantime, the community officially became a town and even served briefly as a county seat. Washington County, created in March 1836 by the Convention, officially organized in December 1837. The Congress of the Republic approved a bill for the incorporation of Crockett, Houston, Refugio, and Washington in June 1837, and on December 12, 1837, all four towns were incorporated. The building where the Convention met, which had become known as Independence Hall, became the town hall and county courthouse, though it also served as a store as it passed through the hands of various owners.[37]

Washington County as originally created from Washington municipality was very large; ultimately eight additional counties would be carved from it. The first was Navasota County in January 1841, and the legislation that created it mandated that the seat of Washington County had to be within three miles of the geographic center of the new boundaries. Mount Vernon, a community surveyed that same year, became the new seat before the close of 1841. Washington residents complained bitterly; an editorial in the *National Vindicator*, published in their town, echoed their protests about the "inconvenience, and the grievous evils arising from the situation of the present county seat—destitute as it is of everything that can facilitate the distribution of justice." A petition was submitted to the Texas Congress, which in January 1844 authorized an election to select a new seat. When Mount Vernon and Turkey Creek dropped out of the race, it became a choice between another new community, Brenham, and Independence. The former outpolled the latter by three votes in February 1844, two months before lots went on sale at the new county seat.[38]

For years after the Revolution, Washington promoters pressed for the return of the Texas national government to their town. The Congress of the Republic of Texas met at Columbia, which boasted both a press and a central location, in the fall of 1836 by order of President David G. Burnet. Thomas Gay made a strong pitch for Washington when the congressmen discussed the location for their next meeting, but his proposal polled second to another resolution that named Houston as the next capital. Asa Hoxey and others continued to lobby for Washington with the support of Sam Houston, who during his second term as the president of the Republic became disgruntled when the government moved to Austin. In March 1842 he got a reason to return to Washington when a small Mexican army raided San Antonio. He ordered Congress to meet at Houston during June 1842, and then mandated a move to Washington when there was a second Mexican raid on San Antonio in September 1842. His decision was facilitated by an offer from Washington attorney William Y. McFarland, who conveyed terms in the summer of 1842 that included free offices for Congress and other Republic officials, who paid thousands of dollars each year to the town of Houston for facilities.[39]

Ironically, when Congress arrived in Washington, many people who had lobbied for the government's return were absent. The San Antonio raid in September 1842 greatly alarmed the residents. Men and boys hastily prepared for a campaign, and soon most of them left in small groups to fight the raiders. Even those who did not march contributed to the cause: planters at Washington pledged bales of cotton to be sold to support the troops. Houston in early October appointed Alexander Somervell to lead the expedition, and ultimately about two-thirds of the Washington County militia joined him. Hundreds of volunteers passed through Washington on their way west, and Houston gave a stirring speech to one detachment, urging them to fight to the death and never surrender. By early November twelve hundred Texans were with Somervell, of whom

Alexander Somervell and Wife, Cornelia Olivia (Sewell) Somervell. From Franklin Keagy, *A History of the Kägy Relationship in America* (Harrisburg, Pa.: Harrisburg Publishing Company, 1899).

three hundred were from Washington County. They organized into two regiments; one, the First Regiment of the Second Brigade, was under the command of Col. James R. Cook, who had married John A. Lott's daughter, Sarah Ann. Cook had four companies led by captains with Washington ties: Phillip H. Coe; William S. Fisher; Jerome B. Robertson, who had been mayor of Washington in 1839; and Elijah S. C. Robertson. Jesse L. McCrocklin, who had served with James G. Swisher in 1835 and William W. Hill in 1836 and brought most of the Washington County militia to join Somervell, became Cook's lieutenant colonel, then led the Second Regiment of the First Brigade, and finally served as a paymaster. Elsewhere, Swisher also commanded a company, and Samuel Bogart, a recent arrival from Missouri in Washington County, had a spy company.[40]

Somervell's force began to dissolve as he marched south in pursuit of the Mexican raiders. Conflicts emerged, especially over the question of whether to cross the Rio Grande, and many volunteers, including most of those from Washington County, quit. Jerome B. Robertson, along with McCrocklin, led two hundred men home. Sterling B. Hendricks of Washington was in Bogart's company, and he and many of his colleagues followed Swisher home. Cook resigned in anger at one point, but he was persuaded to stay and was elected to command the Second Brigade. Fisher became the commander of the First Regiment, so Claudius Buster took charge of his company. When Somervell ordered his remaining troops back to San Antonio, many defied him. Led by Fisher, hundreds occupied, abandoned, and then attempted to recapture the Mexican town of Mier. Exhaustion led them to surrender, and they were sent to Perote Prison. Some died trying to escape, while others were executed in retaliation for these operations in what became infamous as the Mier Expedition. Brenham, the new seat of Washington County, was named in honor of Richard F. Brenham, a veteran of the 1841 Santa Fe Expedition who followed Buster to Mier and then was killed while trying to escape. Jesse Farral of Washington, who donated part of the site for Brenham, insisted upon naming the town for his friend. Fisher and Buster were among those who were released and returned to Texas, but others apparently decided that they had enough. For example, Fisher's assistant surgeon, William F. McMath of Washington, moved to Alabama after he was freed.[41]

While Somervell's men quarreled among themselves, similar conflicts over the move to Washington emerged among the political leaders of the Republic of Texas. Anson Jones later grumbled that Houston made the decision "in a fit of Executive spleen." Charles Elliot, assigned by the British government to represent them, declared that Houston was compelled to move the government by "feuds and jealousies." Houston had ordered the relocation without the approval of his Congress, and they responded spitefully. It was ten days before a quorum assembled at the new capital in November 1842, and a resolution to return to Austin was only narrowly defeated. Austin residents rallied to defend their town's status. Someone tried to shoot Thomas W. Ward, the commissioner of the General Land Office, reportedly because he was a supporter of Houston, and when Houston sent some men to bring the land records to Washington, they were foiled in a confrontation that became infamous as the "Archive War." The materials were not moved to Washington until 1844.[42]

Thomas W. Ward. From Homer S. Thrall, *A Pictorial History of Texas* (St. Louis: N. D. Thompson & Company, 1879).

Much opposition to Washington lay in the fact that it was still not very developed and might be unhealthy. Elliot described the town as having "12 or 13 Wooden shanties," adding that it was accessible only by an "ox train" or packhorses. He declared that even Houston had found Washington to be "rather raw." Later Elliot wrote to Jones that Washington was both unsafe and "very unhealthy." Prince Carl of Solms-Braunfels, who visited the town while trying to establish a colony, agreed that it "must be the most miserable and unhealthy place in Texas." Washington certainly was no more unsafe or unhealthy than any other Texas town in the

1840s, but it was not entirely free of problems. Influenza erupted during early 1845, claiming the lives, among others, of Sen. John W. Smith, who had survived the Alamo as a courier, and Rep. Gustavus W. Parker, a Houston supporter who had previously served in the Texas Senate. Both died in January 1845, and Smith was hurriedly buried in Washington rather than returned to San Antonio. Another victim may have been John W. Hall, the founder of Washington who worked as a clerk in the Post Office of the Republic. He died in early January 1845, and both houses of the Texas Congress adjourned to attend his funeral.[43]

One problem with Washington as a seat of government in 1836 had been the lack of a press, but that had been corrected by late 1842. William W. Gant and Andrew J. Greer issued a prospectus in early 1836 for a newspaper, the *Texas Reporter,* to be published at Washington, but the Runaway Scrape ended their production after a few issues. When the Convention ordered one thousand copies of the Texas Declaration of Independence to be printed, it had to be done in San Felipe. John Warren J. Niles began publishing the *Texas Emigrant* at Washington in July 1839. It lasted a little more than a year, and Niles stored his press in an empty house. Baptist minister Anderson Buffington and his partner, Foster Brigance, salvaged Niles's equipment and started the *Tarantula* during the spring of 1841. Always short of money, Buffington often had to forage for scrap paper to print his newspaper, and he quit in early 1842. Greenberry H. Harrison brought his press to Washington from Austin in June 1842, changing the name of his paper from the *Texian* to the *Texian and Brazos Farmer.* He sold his press to Thomas J. "Ramrod" Johnson in November 1842. Johnson, who earned his nickname with strongly worded attacks on editors who criticized Houston, renamed his newspaper the *National Vindicator* in June 1843, with the motto of "Our Country—our whole country—and nothing but our country." Poor health forced him to take a brief hiatus, but he resumed working, with the support of Washington D. Miller and William H. Cushney, and continued until late 1844, after Jones became president. Johnson also was active in politics, serving as county judge, advocate general in the trial of Edwin V. Moore of the Texas Navy, and chair of the caucus in Brenham that chose the Washington County delegates to the annexation convention. When he stopped publishing his newspaper, Miller and Cushney began producing the *Texas National Register* at Washington in December 1844.[44]

Clever opponents of moving the national government to Washington might have noted that conflicts between settlers and Indians in the area had not yet been resolved, but Houston as president took decisive steps on this matter. He dispatched George W. Terrell to meet with the representatives of the Caddos, Wichitas, and others gathered on Tehuacana Creek in March 1843. Terrell endorsed a treaty with them, and then some followed him back to Washington, camping about a mile from town. Houston talked with them in April 1843, pressing hard for more treaties that would keep whites and Indians separate by moving the latter further west, thus hopefully reducing conflict. The president made quite an impression, wearing a long red gown given to him by the Sultan of Turkey. During the meetings, which lasted twelve days, many townspeople visited the Indian camp, and a dance was held as well as a banquet. One Anglo woman recalled many years later that she was mesmerized by the dancing of thirty or so young Indian women. Townspeople even allowed Indians to stay in vacant homes in Washington. Yet another council followed in the summer of 1843, which brought a second visit to Washington by Indian families in March 1844. Houston again met with the leaders while curious Indians and Anglos mingled freely. After a conference during the fall of 1844 on Tehuacana Creek, where more agreements were signed, Indians did not come again to Washington. Local newspapers still reported Indian attacks, but they occurred relatively far away.[45]

The political leaders of the Republic in the 1840s did struggle to find living and working space in Washington, just as they did in 1836. Locals shared their homes, while hastily prepared quarters, some admittedly shacks, were used for offices. Houston and his wife, Margaret, who gave birth to their first son at Washington in May 1843, stayed with Judge John Lockhart and his family. Houston's presidential office was a tiny one-room building formerly used by lawyer Wilson Y. McFarland. He shared the cramped space with his secretary, Washington D. Miller. The General Land Office settled in a house with no glass in its windows, a leaky roof, and no stove for warmth. Jones ran the State Department in a remodeled carpenter's shop, using rags in place of proper chinking when cold winds blew. Both houses of Congress sometimes met in Independence Hall, but the Senate also worked in the store formerly owned by Edward Bailey, Asa Hoxey, and Thomas Gay, and in the hotel Nathaniel Norwood purchased from Stephen R. Roberts about 1844. When the legislators had money, they paid $150 to meet in the upstairs room of Basil M. Hatfield's Alhambra, a saloon and grocery. His building was the largest in town, and he removed his interior stairs and built exterior ones to give the congressmen direct access and to keep some of them from slipping away to the downstairs bar. As an observer noted, "There is but little liquor in town; but nevertheless it finds its way to the lips of some of the Honorable members." This arrangement almost led to a tragedy during Jones's inaugural ball in 1845, when a woman escorted by Thomas Jefferson Chambers fell through the opening where the inside stairs had been removed.[46]

Becoming the capital of the Republic of Texas in the fall of 1842 brought an economic revival to Washington. Merchants and craftsmen jostled for space with lawyers and doctors, as well as politicians. The Washington *National Vindicator* in December 1843 declared that "the bustle of waggons [*sic*] and carts and general appearance of business, imparted an interest to our town we have never witnessed before." Editor Washington D. Miller and publisher William H. Cushney, in the initial edition of their *Texas National Register* one year later, praised the high level of activity in Washington, where new buildings had been constructed and accommodations made to correct the complaints of the legislators. They happily reported that their town had five stores, as well as lodgings for visitors. A popular guide to Texas claimed that Washington in 1845 had 1,200 people, a rapid increase over just half a decade earlier. Obviously, the removal of the capital to Austin that year led to the departure of some businessmen. Nathaniel Norwood, for example, bought Roberts's hotel in 1844 and sold it in 1845. Miller and Cushney also moved to Austin, but before leaving they repeated a mantra popular with many Washington promoters: "The navigation of the [Brazos] river by steam will soon repair any loss which such removal may seem, for the moment, to produce."[47]

For many years the only regular method of transportation that linked Washington to the outside world was stage lines. Mail contractors operated in town beginning in 1837, offering a ride to Houston in thirty-six hours and to Richmond, seventy miles away, in twenty-eight hours. By 1844 the Houston trip had been reduced to thirty hours, although the journey was still made only once a week. The long hours were not the worst part of the travel experience. George W. Kendall, editor of the New Orleans *Picayune* and a veteran of the disastrous Santa Fe Expedition in 1841, traveled by stagecoach and horse from Houston to Washington in the spring of 1845 with several other travelers. He remembered: "swimming, digging, floundering from Houston to this place, two days of the time completely weather and water bound . . . it is not altogether so simple to swim a vehicle . . . , nor is it easy to drag it through the deep, heavy, black mud of the prairies." He was lucky; sometimes floodwaters washed away the roads, or even swept the Washington ferry downstream with a stage on board.[48]

After the Texas Revolution, the ambitions of Washington investors focused on the *Yellowstone*, a steamer built in Kentucky for the Missouri River fur trade. It had proven unsuited for that work and was brought to Texas by Samuel May Williams and Thomas F. McKinney, who had other plans for it. The side-wheeler measured 122 feet long and just over twenty feet wide, and in the hands of a careful master could make its way along Texas rivers. John E. Ross earned a measure of immortality when he ferried Sam Houston and his army across the Brazos in April 1836, during the Runaway Scrape. By the fall of 1836 the *Yellowstone* was making regular runs up and down the Brazos between Washington and Quintana, where larger vessels loaded cargo for the trip to Galveston or Houston. But early hopes were dashed when the steamboat foundered in Buffalo Bayou in 1837. Editor John Warren J. Niles of the *Texas Emigrant* called a town meeting at Washington in the late summer of 1839 that offered bounties to steamer captains bold enough to come upriver, but the landing remained quiet for almost six years.[49]

Commercial ambitions resurged in 1842 with the dramatic arrival of the *Mustang* at Washington. The steamer was constructed that year as a ferryboat to operate at Galveston, but its owners were lured up the Brazos by unusually high water. As Capt. John Singer brought his boat into the landing at Washington under a full head of steam, pushing back against the strong current, his engineer suddenly released the pressure through an exhaust pipe with a loud blast that panicked people and animals alike. Singer subsequently made his way past Hidalgo Falls up to Port Sullivan before returning downriver, carrying both freight and travelers. The *Mustang*

Early Texas Steamboat. From Carol Belanger Grafton (ed), *Ready-to Use Old-Fashioned Transportations Cuts* (Mineola, N. Y.: Dover, 1987), 25, and found at www.maritimetexas.net.

made several trips to Washington in late 1842 and early 1843, hauling 253 bales of cotton and nine passengers down the Brazos on one run. Greed proved its ruin: overloaded in November 1843, it sank at its mooring downriver from Washington. Plans to raise and repair it did not result in its return to service on the Brazos.[50]

The colorfully named *Lady Byron* replaced the *Mustang* at Washington, arriving just weeks after the loss of the latter boat. Battling "strong currents and driftwood," the *Lady Byron*, captained by Stephen W. Tichenor, unloaded nine hundred barrels of freight at Washington on December 11, 1843, and steamed downriver the next day for Velasco. Tichenor and John H. Sterrett had originally bought the boat to use on the Trinity River, but they sold the *Lady Byron* earlier in 1843 to Greenberry H. Harrison, who must have been pleased when the trip proved to be "much more profitable . . . than expected." He personally brought the steamboat upriver to Washington in January 1844, but the *Lady Byron* hit a snag and sank below Richmond on the Brazos on its downriver run. After lying on the river bottom for about a year, the *Lady Byron* was raised and refurbished by Tichenor and Sterrett, only to be wrecked on the bar at Velasco in 1845.[51]

While Washington businessmen struggled to develop their town, the most important issue debated by the Texas Congresses at Washington was joining the United States. Editor Miller of the Washington *Texas National Register*, Houston's former secretary, railed against annexation, warning that the "demon spirit of ABOLITIONISM" was ascendant in American politics, but few listened to him. Washington County, like most of the Republic, had overwhelmingly voted for annexation in 1836, and in the spring of 1845 a "mass meeting" at Washington once more endorsed joining the United States and asked that Jones convene Congress to decide the issue. The legislators gathered in June 1845 and unanimously approved annexation, providing for a convention to meet the next month in Austin. In short order, the convention delegates accepted annexation, wrote a state constitution, and officially petitioned to join the Union. Semiweekly mail service from Washington to Austin was established to bring news of the convention as regularly as possible. The arrival of seven companies of the Second United States Dragoons at Washington in August 1845, months before the people of Texas or the U.S. Congress approved annexation, made it clear that Texas in many ways was already a part of the United States.[52]

One of the last measures passed by the Annexation Convention in August 1845 provided that the new state government would be in Austin. Government offices in Washington closed for the last time on October 4, 1845, and clerks began packing for the move west. John S. Ford had led the faction in the last regular meeting of the Texas Congress that hotly opposed moving the capital to Austin, arguing that the frontier town was too exposed to Indian attacks to be a safe place for government or archives, but they had lost the vote. Their final stand was undermined by Jones, who as president did not oppose the western legislators who pushed for their town to be the state capital of Texas. The last act by Jones as the president of the Republic of Texas, a transfer of authority to James P. Henderson as the new governor, took place in a ceremony at Austin, not Washington.[53]

The annexation of Texas by the United States, and the related disagreement over the Rio Grande as a boundary, led to conflict with Mexico, and again Washington volunteers joined the fight.

Anson Jones. From Homer S. Thrall, *A Pictorial History of Texas* (St. Louis: N. D. Thompson & Company, 1879).

The federal government in 1846 asked for four regiments of riflemen to be mustered in Texas, two of which were to be mounted. By mid-June, more than one thousand men passed through Washington on their way to Mexico. Among them were the members of a mounted company raised in Washington County and two foot companies enrolled in Washington and Brazos Counties. Company F of the First Texas Mounted Riflemen, commanded by Col. John C. Hays, mustered in Washington County in June 1846 and served for four months. In September several members of the company were wounded when Hays's Texans participated in the hard fighting that accompanied the capture of Monterrey. The federal government called for two thousand more Texas volunteers in early 1847, and Hays enlisted another regiment, the First Texas Mounted Volunteers (Twelve Months). Company G from Washington County mustered into this regiment in May 1847 and followed Colonel Hays to Mexico City, where they fought both regulars and partisans while a treaty to end the war was being debated. Of the 115 officers and men in this company, 19 died in service before Company G returned home in May 1848 and disbanded.[54]

As Texas became a state, then, Washington residents could claim that they had played a major role in the creation of both the Republic of Texas and the Lone Star State. They had fought both Mexicans and Indians on behalf of Texas. Their fledgling town had twice been the seat of government for the Republic, the Texas Declaration of Independence and first constitution had been written in their community, and the annexation of Texas as a state had been endorsed at Washington. While the capital of the new state was at Austin, and efforts to remain a county seat had failed, Washington had made great progress in developing its commercial sector and social institutions. Community leaders believed that, if they could further expand upon Washington's role as a river port for steamers, their town would not only endure but prosper.

Chapter 3

COMMERCIAL CENTER

Washington was originally established as a business venture, and arguably it nearly succeeded. After a hard stumble in the late 1830s, the town stabilized during the next decade, and it boomed during the early 1850s. The population of Texas almost tripled from 1850 to 1860, and Washington County followed suit, becoming the second most populous county in Texas on the eve of the Civil War. Market agriculture fueled economic growth during the same period, and Washington County ranked among the top cotton-producing counties in the state, which also made it one of the wealthiest counties in Texas. Slaves provided much of the labor needed for such production, and blacks outnumbered whites in Washington County by the eve of the Civil War.[55] Washington, as a landing for steamers carrying cotton downriver and consumer goods upriver, benefited from this economic boom, but local leaders struggled to maintain law and order in a period of rapid change.

Washington profited in part from several antebellum efforts to improve travel on the Brazos River. A lot of debate, and some work, focused on two points: removing snags in the channel from the river's mouth to Washington and shortening the trip to Galveston by digging a canal from just above the mouth of the river to the western end of Galveston Bay. Greenberry H. Harrison spent sixteen days on the *Pioneer* on the Brazos in 1847 and 1848, surveying the river from Washington to the Gulf of Mexico. He reported that it would take $4,000 to clear snags and remove shoals. The Brazos River Steam Association, of which he was a member, discussed raising the money to remove the obstructions, but the organization collapsed financially in the early 1850s. A United States Army lieutenant surveyed the same water in 1854 and declared it would actually take $50,000 to clear the Brazos. The legislature in 1856 appropriated $300,000 to improve the state's navigable rivers, including the $50,000 recommended for the Brazos. John M. Brown and Richard French of Washington got the Brazos River contract and during 1857 made some progress in clearing both snags and shoals. Additional state money was set aside for more work, but the war intervened.[56]

Those who wanted a canal from the Brazos River mouth to Galveston also had to settle for partial success. Stephen F. Austin suggested a canal to link the lower Brazos with Galveston Bay as early as 1825, and the Texas Congress chartered the Brazos Canal Company in 1841 for this task. Not much happened, and in 1850 a new outfit, the Galveston and Brazos Navigation Company, received a state charter. It had the authority to raise $150,000 by subscription (or up to double that amount if necessary), the right to charge tolls, and the power of eminent domain. Joseph H. Wood directed the fund-raising in Washington, while the list of other fund-raisers included Laird M. H. Butler of Galveston. Money proved hard to find, and contractor David Bradbury completed only one mile of the canal by 1853. That February the legislature tried to expedite several projects by providing more money and appointing three-man boards to oversee each waterway, but the proposal had to be approved in a popular referendum. Washington voted 159 to 3 in favor of the bill, but the rest of the county joined the state majority in rejecting it. Undaunted, Washington leaders met during 1854 and 1855 to raise money to support further construction. By the close of 1855, the canal was completed at a cost of $340,000. Eight miles long, fifty feet wide, and less than four feet deep, it was never satisfactory. Discussions of improvements yielded no further results before the Civil War.[57]

While the debates concerning river projects continued, steamboat investor Stephen W. Tichenor resumed his operations on the Brazos River in 1847 with the *Samuel May Williams*, which at least one local historian later declared was the "largest, best equipped and most elegant vessel that has ever done service on this stream." The side-wheeler was 135 feet in length, had a beam of just over 27 feet, and was built for Tichenor and Thomas F. McKinney to use in the coast trade. But they moved the *Samuel May Williams* into the Brazos, where in April 1848 Capt. Joseph Emerson hit a sandbar above San Felipe during an attempt to push upriver. Trying again the next month, Emerson steamed to Washington and returned triumphantly to Galveston. There the steamboat operated for almost another year before a storm wrecked it in April 1849.[58]

Economic hopes revived in Washington with the emergence of a new organization. A few months before the *Samuel May Williams* was lost at Galveston, two new steamboats arrived at Washington: the *Washington,* captained by James E. Haviland, and the *Brazos,* with Tichenor proudly at the helm. The Brazos River Steam Association, a joint stock company organized at Washington in 1844 with local and Galveston investors, owned both vessels. Among the local investors were Greenberry H. Harrison and Richard R. Peebles, who arranged the steamboats' construction with relatives in Ohio. Joseph H. Wood served as secretary for the company and its agent at Washington. In Galveston, the primary investors were two brothers, George and Laird M. H. Butler. The latter served as president of the company and supervised the actual building of the steamers at Pittsburgh. As finished, each was 120 feet long and 22 feet wide, with berths for passengers and cargo holds for hundreds of cotton bales. Both had double boilers, with stern wheels thirteen feet in diameter and seventeen feet wide. Best of all, they allegedly could float in just fifteen inches of water. Apparently they were also nicely fitted; at least one traveler was "impressed" with the "stately commons, fancy windows and glass doors" of the *Washington.*[59]

Despite the snide comments of Houston editors, investment in the two steamers quickly began to pay off as hundreds of bales of cotton traveled down the Brazos. The pair carried 1,200 bales downriver in January 1849, and the *Washington* carried 715 bales in one run to Velasco in February. Not to be outdone, Capt. William Brentling brought the *Brazos* to the same port in March with 562 bales along with 128 sacks and 4 barrels of pecans. The *Brazos* stuck on the shoals at Richmond when river trade resumed during the fall of 1849, but she was soon back in operation. A Houston editor noted that Brazos steamboats had brought the price of transport on the river down 20 percent in just one year, and he admitted that his town was profiting from the cotton they brought downriver and the goods they carried upriver. The high point for the Brazos River Steam Association came in the spring of 1850, when Brentling, on the *Brazos,* competed with Hatfield, who cap-

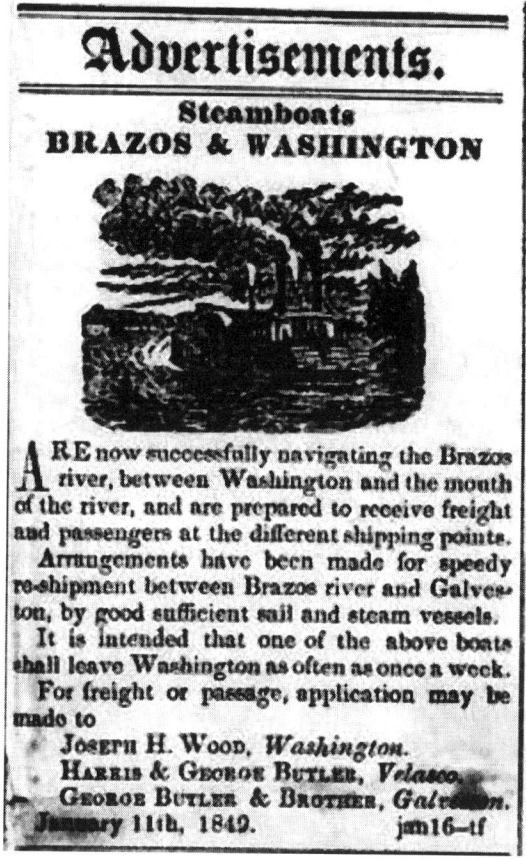

Advertisements.

Steamboats
BRAZOS & WASHINGTON

ARE now successfully navigating the Brazos river, between Washington and the mouth of the river, and are prepared to receive freight and passengers at the different shipping points.

Arrangements have been made for speedy re-shipment between Brazos river and Galveston, by good sufficient sail and steam vessels.

It is intended that one of the above boats shall leave Washington as often as once a week.

For freight or passage, application may be made to

JOSEPH H. WOOD, *Washington.*
HARRIS & GEORGE BUTLER, *Velasco.*
GEORGE BUTLER & BROTHER, *Galveston.*
January 11th, 1849.   jan16–tf

Advertisement from *Texas Ranger and Brazos Guard,* Jan. 1, 1849.

tained the *Washington.* High water floated the *Brazos* to Munson's Bluff, about one hundred miles above Washington on the Brazos River. Not to be outdone, Hatfield took the *Washington* to within two miles of Cameron, on the Little River. It was the only time a steamboat ever reached Cameron. Hatfield hosted a three-day party to celebrate his feat, and many years later a historical marker was placed to record it.[60]

Bad business decisions led to financial losses for the Brazos River Steam Association, and so Washington investors sold their interests in the two steamers to the Butler brothers of Galveston. Perhaps the hardest hit was Wood, who also sold most of a league of land along the Brazos River to Laird M. H. Butler. He watched helplessly when his home burned, afterward declaring personal bankruptcy. After the sale, the *Brazos* made one more run to Washington in June 1851, and then was put to work with the *Washington* on the Trinity River. More than two years passed before the *Brazos* returned to Washington, while its counterpart was reportedly abandoned in 1854. Purchased by Robert and David G. Mills and refurbished, the *Brazos* churned up and down its namesake river in 1854 under the command of Harrison, Hatfield (who thus was the only man to captain both the *Brazos* and *Washington*), John C. Walker, and William Jenkins. The steamer went as far upriver as the new town of Port Sullivan (with Hatfield at the helm), carrying cotton, groceries, and other merchandise. It left Washington for the last time in April 1857, hauling 595 bales of cotton to Galveston.[61]

Wood's financial collapse led to one of the stranger financial ventures launched from antebellum Washington. Reports of a gold strike near the Guadalupe Mountains in early 1853 prompted about fifty men to leave in a group for the alleged goldfields in West Texas. Editor Joseph Lancaster sarcastically noted upon their return in about six months that "They saw gold, but neglected to bring any home." He added mysteriously, "they also saw the elephant," which may indicate that some of them had fought with Indians or fellow adventurers. The idea of easy wealth persisted, and in May 1856 Wood led another group west to work in the silver mines being dug in southern New Mexico near Las Cruces, close to El Paso. Wood, who also hoped to find some gold and even tried digging for lead, settled in the Organ Mountains and persisted long after most of his companions returned home. Finally he quit and came back to Washington in early 1857 without finding any treasure.[62]

While Wood left the Brazos trade by 1850, other captains tried their luck at Washington, lured by periodic high water, the withdrawal of the *Washington* and *Brazos* to the Trinity River, or the bad fortune of their maritime rivals. Jenkins brought the steamer *Elite* upriver during high water in February 1850. A stern-wheeler built in Pennsylvania, 114 feet in length, it returned to Washington in March with William Montgomery at the helm. He took his boat further upriver in June, but it was later sent to the Trinity River, where it sank in March 1852. Horace Baldwin also took advantage of high water in 1850, arriving at Washington in June on the

Jack Hays, which carried 1,500 barrels of "government stores." His plan was to establish a military depot as far up the Brazos as possible, hopefully in Waco Village or even further. Washington residents did not profit from the enterprise, and the *Jack Hays* did not come again. It, too, was sent to the Trinity, where it sank in December 1853. High water came again during the spring of 1852 and brought the *Camden*, a relatively small stern-wheeler assembled in Pennsylvania and piloted to Texas by Capt. William C. Smith. He battled driftwood as he made his way past Washington to Port Sullivan, and then lost his boat to a snag near San Felipe in April 1852. The *Reliance,* a side-wheeler built in Ohio and captained by Frederick A. Maffitt, followed the *Camden* to Port Sullivan in May 1852 and brought five hundred bales downriver, despite being briefly stranded. Maffitt never tried that again. The steamer *Buffalo* also operated on the Brazos in the spring of 1852, traveling to Washington and as much as 120 miles above it.[63]

Two new steamers reached Washington during the fall of 1852: *Major A. Harris* with Captain Jenkins and *William Penn* with Capt. J. W. Sleepier. The first was built at Cincinnati and brought to Texas by Henry L. Kinney as part of his development plans for Corpus Christi. It proved unsuited for the rough waters of the bay, so it was sold and relocated. It carried cotton, hides, and groceries to and from Washington, and then was wrecked when both boilers exploded as it tried to push through the canal dug from the lower Brazos to Galveston Bay in February 1857. The *William Penn*, another Ohio-built side-wheeler, had foundered in the coastal trade in 1851 but had been raised and refitted. Her bad luck continued on her first run above Washington, when the steamer was trapped above Hidalgo Falls for almost two months. Ironically the town of William Penn, near Hidalgo Falls, was allegedly named for the boat. Capt. William Pool was apparently in command when the *William Penn* struck a snag near San Felipe in May 1854 and "sank to her wheelhouses." Hundreds of cotton bales were salvaged, but the boat was lost.[64]

Low water levels apparently kept some steamers from reaching Washington in 1853, but at least one did make it to the landing. Capt. John C. Wallis brought the steamer *Magnolia* up the Brazos to Warren, just a few miles below Washington, carried a full load of cotton back down, and then returned and loaded cotton bales at Washington. The *Magnolia* had originally been constructed for George Butler in Pennsylvania three years earlier under the direction of James E. Haviland. It was 130 feet long and 24 feet wide, and it allegedly could carry 1,100 bales of cotton. Sent to the Trinity River originally, it was sold in an auction in early 1852 and was then transferred to the Brazos. After making two trips to the Washington area in 1853, it returned in 1855 to the Trinity.[65]

The apparently unstoppable Harrison landed at Warren and Washington in April 1854 aboard the steamer *Nick Hill*. A small stern-wheeler, built in Buffalo Bayou in 1851 and named for Nicholas S. Hilliard, who owned a billiard parlor in Galveston, the *Nick Hill* had been almost destroyed by a boiler explosion on its first run, and then sank in the Trinity River in 1853. Harrison bought it not long after that accident, presumably for a very reasonable price, and brought it to Washington with a crew that consisted of him, an engineer, a fireman, and one deckhand. He was the first to take his steamer through the canal from the Brazos River to Galveston, though since it was not quite completed, he did run aground at least once. The little craft's luck ran out at Galveston in October 1854, when it was wrecked by a hurricane.[66]

The development of Washington as a river port provided plenty of material for two newspaper editors in the community. When the state government moved to Austin in 1845, William H. Cushney and Washington D. Miller followed with their *Texas National Register*. Almost four years later, Joseph Lancaster, a Massachusetts native who first came to Washington as an army volunteer in 1836, returned in January 1849 and began publishing the *Texas Ranger and Brazos Guard*. Interestingly, when he was absent, his wife, Eva, also from Massachusetts, wrote material and set type. Their rival was George W. Crawford, a Mississippian who planned to issue a paper at Washington in 1848 but stepped aside when Lancaster arrived. Perhaps not happy with Lancaster's production, Crawford bought the *Lone Star* from its Brenham publishers in 1850 and moved the paper to Washington, where it appeared as the *Semi-Weekly Star* with William H. Ewing, the former schoolmaster and chief justice of Washington County, as editor. Within a year Ewing was gone and Crawford had a new partner, Daniel H. Rankin, and a new title, *Lone Star and Southern Watch Tower*. In the summer of 1852 Crawford sold his share of the business to Rankin, who

Masthead of *Texas Ranger and Lone Star,* October 15, 1853

briefly worked with J. W. Wynne as editor before the "subscription books" were sold to Lancaster in October 1852. Rankin established another paper in Brenham and Crawford tried publishing in Austin, while Lancaster endured a disastrous fire but continued to publish his *Texas Ranger and Lone Star* in Washington.[67]

Lancaster, one of the most active promoters of trade on the Brazos River, declared his community's emancipation in 1849 from the exploitive monopoly of Houston, whose "history of repeated injuries, oppressions, and extortions" included sending its "old and rotten steamboats into the Brazos river, to be sunk for the benefit of the underwriters." While the records of the Brazos steamers during the first decade after annexation do not entirely support Lancaster's bold declaration, commerce did transform Washington during this era, mostly for the better. Frank Brown in a memoir noted that steamers brought new life to Washington. A local correspondent wrote to a friend in 1849: "The boats have commenced running and the hammers are knocking. There are some 8 or 10 new buildings going up at this place now." A popular guide to Texas echoed the same theme: "The recent improvements in the navigation of the river have given a new impulse to business, and the town is in a rapid state of improvement, and bids fair to become one of the most important towns in Texas."[68]

Perhaps a thousand people lived in Washington by 1852. The Galveston *Weekly Journal* reported that, in addition to merchants and ever-present saloon keepers such as Basil M. Hatfield, there were "a dozen or less, each, of lawyers and physicians." A writer for the *Texas Ranger and Lone Star* was not so happy about that.

While he refrained from ugly comments about doctors, he wrote that lawyers were "as thick as mosquitoes, and fully as thirsty." Conversely, another correspondent in the same newspaper one year later complained that Washington's doctors were becoming "loafers" because the climate was so healthy that people were not getting yellow fever and other maladies as they did elsewhere. Several brick buildings had been built or were under construction, including a market hall. One of the largest edifices was the Alhambra Saloon and Restaurant, while the three-story Austin House hotel, completed by Robert A. Lott in 1854, may have been larger. Joseph H. Wood and Isaac Thayer also had hotels during this period, while others made their living as pharmacists, dentists, tinsmiths, gunsmiths, shoemakers, jewelers, saddlers, photographers, watchmakers, and blacksmiths. The community enjoyed daily mail service to Chappell Hill, with mail coming and going to other places several times each week. In sum, steamboats were "doing a swimming business," and so was Washington, whose optimism was expressed in an editorial in the *Texas Ranger and Lone Star,* which declared that the town had a "fine, beautiful, convenient and healthy location, and nothing but the total want of unity, exertion, and public spirit can prevent it from being a fine, thrifty business place."[69]

Life in antebellum Washington was more than just business—social organizations grew as the town prospered. The most prominent associations were the Masons. Together, Washington Lodge No. 18 (Scottish Rite) and Washington Chapter No. 5 (York Rite) invited the Texas Grand Lodge in 1847 to settle in their planned new two-story brick Masonic Hall, with a lower level to be used as a school or market and an upper level hosting Masonic functions. The Grand Lodge declined the offer, but the Grand Chapter of Texas did meet in the new building at Washington in 1853. By the summer of 1856, Brazos Chapter No. 9 of the Royal Arch Masons (York Rite) organized in Washington, giving the community a full complement of Masonic organizations on the eve of the Civil War.[70]

Henry R. Cartmell, a prominent Washington Mason who became treasurer of the Texas Grand Lodge in 1857, also became a chair, or Noble Grand, for the International Order of Odd Fellows (IOOF) in Washington. There were two IOOF organizations in town: Starr Lodge No. 22 and Anson Jones Encampment No. 4. The latter welcomed only those who had passed through the third degree of a lodge, so it was a higher order. Cartmell presided over a celebration in August 1854, when a brass band led members wearing formal regalia in a parade from their lodge to Ruter Methodist Church. Supper was served at the Washington Hotel, which also hosted a ball that evening. The occasion was the convening of the IOOF Grand Lodge of Texas at Washington for its semiannual "communication." Three years later, Henry E. Lockett of Washington was elected Grand Patriarch of the IOOF Grand Lodge of Texas. Interestingly, there were always close ties between the IOOF and the Masons in the community of Washington. For example, James H. Littlefield served as secretary of Washington Lodge No. 18, of the Scottish Rite Masons in 1856, and filled the same position in 1857 for Starr Lodge No. 22 (IOOF).[71]

As community leaders, Masons became involved in building both churches and schools in Washington. In April 1852, Masons unearthed and reburied Martin Ruter by the foundation for a new brick Methodist church in Washington. They also helped lay the cornerstone, and within a few months William P. Smith reported the completion of a "large and splendid brick church" on the town lots originally acquired by Ruter. Dedicated in Ruter's name, it was described by one visitor as a "large and commodious house for the worship of God." In reality it was about 2,400 square feet, with pews provided by Gabriel Felder, a planter who lived on New Year Creek in Washington County and served as a trustee for Soule University in Chappell Hill. Felder also paid to finish the church belfry in 1853, and a bell originally sent to Washington by Methodist women in Pittsburgh in honor of Ruter was moved from the old church to the new building. Plans were later made to acquire an even larger facility, but apparently the onset of the Civil War interrupted that scheme.[72]

Baptist minister William M. Tryon left Washington for Houston in late 1846, but this time the congregation survived the departure of their minister. When the Texas Baptist State Convention organized in September 1848, Washington was one of twenty-one churches that sent a delegate. Like the Methodists, they built a new brick church in 1852, which enabled them to sell the brick house they had previously used as a chapel. J. B. Stiteler and Noah Hill, both of whom had taught at Baylor University in Independence, were among those who preached in the new Baptist church at Washington in the 1850s. Stiteler was also noted for his work as an editor with the *Texas Baptist*, an influential religious publication in antebellum Texas, while Hill came to Texas in 1847 as part of a group of Baptist missionaries and became well known for his work in preaching to blacks and recruiting Germans into the church (along with Stiteler).[73]

William Y. Allen in 1840 delivered the first Presbyterian services in Washington, along with Daniel Baker, but no church organized before Allen, who briefly served as chaplain for the Texas Congress, left for Kentucky in 1842. John Limber, a Presbyterian minister, came in May 1846. A year later, a series of meetings at the home of Stephen R. Roberts led to the founding of a Presbyterian church in Washington. There were only twelve members, but George C. Red, a local doctor, and William L. Grisham were chosen to serve as the ruling elders, with Limber as pastor. Membership increased and a "small frame church" was built before Limber drowned at New Orleans in 1849. Hugh Wilson, who had briefly served as chaplain for the Texas House five years earlier, then became the pastor for a congregation of twenty-six. The State Presbytery, four ministers and two ruling elders, met in the new church in June 1849. Church leaders convened again at Washington in November 1856 as the State Synod, with thirty-six ministers and five ruling elders attending. The local representative then was the Reverend J. W. Miller, who had succeeded Wilson and would remain in Washington until 1873.[74]

The Episcopalians were the last denomination to build a church in Washington prior to the Civil War. The Reverend Charles Gillette of Christ Church in Houston visited in March 1843 but did not stay. Years later, the Reverend Henry N. Pierce came to Washington County; by May 1850, he had raised $800 for a sanctuary in Washington and organized St. Paul's Episcopal Church. Joseph H. Wood sold property to Pierce, as the rector of St. Paul's, and Wardens Henry Bailey and Anson Jones in December 1851. The church was built with cedar cut on Jones's Barrington estate and was completed in 1854, although it was another eight years before the Reverend Bishop Alexander Gregg consecrated it. The tiny church struggled to pay its bills but continued to focus on growth. Rector Lindsay P. Rucker, who left the Methodist Church and became an Episcopal priest in 1851, issued an appeal along with Jones and Bailey as vestrymen in March 1855 asking for donations to retire their construction debt of $2,000, and in January 1857 the vestry signed a mortgage for their church with Robert and David G. Mills. But land for a college was acquired from Joseph J. Wyatt in 1860, and Gregg in 1863 bought a house for the rector, the Reverend Robert S. Seeley.[75]

Education in antebellum Washington, as in many other Texas communities, remained primarily a private matter. The Texas Declaration of Independence condemned Mexico for not providing public education, and the Texas Congress gave land grants to schools, but little public money was spent on education throughout the Republic years. The state constitution adopted in 1845 provided for the support of education with taxes, and legislation was passed in 1854 for the disbursement of funds from the Compromise of 1850 as part of a Permanent School Fund, but this brought little lasting change. Washington County commissioners created fourteen districts in May 1854; the Washington district had three trustees charged with building schools, hiring teachers, and choosing students for state-paid scholarships. Surviving records indicate that Washington County spent just over $2,800 of state money in 1854 and 1855, or about two dollars per child. Many Texas counties did nothing, and most communities continued to rely on private schools, so the district system was abolished in 1856. The county courts became responsible for disbursing state education funds, and the total spent in Washington County actually fell slightly just before the Civil War, while the number of students increased. In Washington, as elsewhere in Texas, individuals, churches, and organizations such as the Masons continued to teach local children.[76]

The Washington Masonic Academy reopened during the fall of 1847. The principal was Horace B. Hurlbert, who served as the master of Washington Lodge No. 18 before his death from tuberculosis in 1854. He was succeeded in 1851 by C. W. Emmons and B. F. Wilson, who also became master of Lodge No. 18. This duo provided a broad variety of classes in five-month sessions. More interesting, they assumed all costs of operating the academy; Hurlbert had been supervised and paid by the Masons. Lindsay P. Rucker, who had previously taught for the Masons at Washington beginning in 1839, returned to take charge of the academy in January 1852. He was assisted by Thomas W. Morris and Emily S. Limber, the widow of John Limber, the Presbyterian minister at Washington who drowned in 1849. Emily S. Limber apparently had some professional training as a teacher, which must have been most welcome. By this time, the Masons had built their spacious two-story Masonic Hall and Market House, in which Rucker and his staff offered five-month sessions to as many as one hundred students. In early 1853 Rucker continued as principal of the Masonic Academy with Charles E. Tarver in charge of male education, A. E. Bayle of female education, and Lizzie Brittingham directing the Music Department.[77]

After the close of the spring term in 1853, Rucker reported to the annual state convention of the Episcopal Church in Texas that he was ready to open an Episcopal school in Washington, personally contracting for the use of the Masonic Hall. The terms included the Masons being able to send four students per year free of charge to the new academy, while Rucker would settle the debt of the Washington Masonic Academy with the Masons, which amounted to $700. Rucker's Washington Female Seminary began its first term during the summer of 1853, offering academic subjects as well as instruction in music, embroidery, painting, and drawing. Bayle, along with her husband, H. C. Bayle, worked for Rucker through the summer of 1854, as did Brittingham. By the spring of 1855, Rucker had Harriett Pratt and "Miss Dickson" as assistants. He advertised his campus as located in a grove about a mile from town, with a great view of the community and the Brazos River. His efforts proved unsuccessful. Unable to recruit enough students, he resumed his work as a surveyor by the fall of 1855 and left Washington the next year.[78]

Others arrived to fill the gap left by Rucker. S. H. Devore, who had previously taught mathematics at Irving College in Tennessee, opened the Washington Academy for boys in April 1855. He offered two terms of instruction, each of which lasted twenty weeks. He stayed for only a year, but J. E. Robinson and William L. Crowson, an attorney, kept the academy open. They offered a curriculum organized into four courses of study: Primary, Preparatory, Scientific, and Collegiate. Apparently they also did not last long; by 1861, the only school for boys in town was the Washington Male School. The problem for those who tried to operate schools for boys in Washington was competition. The Texas Congress in February 1845 approved a charter for Baylor University, which opened in nearby Independence. Similarly, the Brazos Presbytery organized

Austin College at Washington in June 1849, although it later located at Huntsville and subsequently moved to Sherman. Other private schools for boys, such as Soule University and its predecessors at Chappell Hill, could be found elsewhere in Washington County.[79]

Emily S. Limber, the widow who had previously worked for Rucker, began teaching women in the Presbyterian church at Washington in January 1856. She offered two three-month terms before a summer break, with classes in geography, arithmetic, composition, French, and "higher English branches." When the Washington Female Seminary opened in April 1856, she was listed as an associate principal along with A. C. Hodgman, the wife of the principal, the Reverend Stephen A. Hodgman, who later served as a chaplain in the Union army during the Civil War. Editor W. J. Pendleton of the *Washington American* complained in March 1857 that there was no school for girls in town, indicating that Hodgman had departed, but Tully Kemp opened the Washington Female Academy in Robert A. Lott's hotel a few months later. Kemp, who taught previously in Maryland and South Carolina, had his wife to help with the teaching duties, which included a full list of academic subjects plus drawing, painting, and piano. They moved in 1858 to Brenham. On the eve of the Civil War, two schools for women remained in Washington. The Reverend Robert S. Seeley of St. Paul's Episcopal Church received public funds as the principal of the female academy housed there. Too, the Washington Collegiate Female Institute, which was nondenominational and "purely literary and scientific," was chartered by the Texas legislature in February 1860. Its trustees from nine Masonic lodges included many familiar names such as Lott, Henry R. Cartmell, Basil M. Hatfield, Richard R. Peebles, and George W. Crawford.[80]

Temperance was often a hotly debated topic in antebellum Washington, as in the rest of the country, and it united church leaders with social organizations. Baptist minister Anderson Buffington as the editor of the short-lived *Tarantula* aggressively promoted temperance in his newspaper, as Joseph Lancaster and George W. Crawford also did in their papers. By the fall of 1849 the Sons of Temperance, which had close ties to the Presbyterian Church and the Masons, met weekly in Washington. Allegedly thousands of people attended the Sons of Temperance rally that same year, when Georgia Jenkins presented a banner to the state organization that was received by Rufus C. Burleson, who later married her. Among those who were converted at this event was Robert M. Williamson. He wrote to a friend: "my old friend John Barleycorn died at my hands . . . I have buried him like a gentleman, but without any day of resurrection." The bemused proprietor of the Brazos House, A. B. Fleury, took the opportunity to tell visitors in a timely advertisement that in addition to a plentiful supply of alcoholic beverages and cigars, his saloon had "a good supply of fine lemons, which he has purchased expressly for their benefit, in order to make some of the best lemonade they had ever tasted." Five years later the Cartmell Union Lodge of the Independent Order of Good Samaritans and Daughters of Samaria mustered at Washington to battle "King Alcohol." There were sixty members, including Cartmell, then mayor, and his wife, Mary. Sam Houston and local leader William P. Rogers addressed the state convention that met at Washington during June 1855, in conjunction with their talks at an American Party meeting in town that month. They did have some effect, as the last saloon in Washington allegedly closed in the summer of 1858. But another paper reported at about the same time that the resourceful Joseph H. Wood was producing "whiskey, brandy, rum, and wine" from sorghum.[81]

Rogers was also active in organizing a militia company, the Independence City Guards, at Washington in the spring of 1854. A former officer in the Mississippi Rifles during the war with Mexico who later served as a consul at Veracruz, Rogers came to Washington in 1851. He was elected captain of the Guards and sent a request to Gov. Elisha M. Pease for arms, but there is no record of a response. Many of his men may have joined the Order of the Lone Star of the West, a chapter of which organized at about the same time in Washington. Texans had taken part in filibustering expeditions to Cuba in 1850 and 1851, and in 1854 preparations were again being made for a similar effort. John S. "Rip" Ford met at New Orleans with former Mississippi governor John A. Quitman and others in the "Order of the Lone Star," which was committed to establishing a proslavery republic in Cuba. Ford then organized his Order of the Lone Star of the West. Prominent Texans raised money and recruited men, but official support declined in the wake of public protests against the Ostend Manifesto, which proposed that the United States buy Cuba or use force to take it if Spain

Robert M. Williamson. From Homer S. Thrall, *A Pictorial History of Texas* (St. Louis: N. D. Thompson & Company, 1879).

declined to sell. When Quitman dropped his Cuban scheme, Ford and most Texans did the same. In Washington, more than one hundred men joined the organization, laid plans for a school for boys, and held a parade and ball on July 4, 1854, but not much more was done. When Pease called for volunteers to fight Indians in the fall, the muster in Washington had to be canceled due to yellow fever. Rogers later moved to Houston, whence he was elected to the Secession Convention. He was killed while leading the Second Texas Infantry in 1862 at Corinth, in his native Mississippi.[82]

The arts also briefly flourished in Washington during the decade prior to the Civil War. An acting company of young men organized in town during early 1851, and within a few years there was a

Thespian Hall. Both local organizations, such as the Washington Histrionic Society, and traveling shows, such as the Star State Minstrels, performed there. A ball was held in July 1856 to raise money for the "LeGrand Library Association," which began meeting at Robert A. Lott's Austin House hotel. The organization was named for W. T. LeGrand, a physician and prominent Mason in Washington who served on its finance committee. Editors Crawford and Pendleton were among the other officers, while the list of members included other Masons who served as trustees for the Washington Female Collegiate Institute when it was chartered by the Texas legislature on Valentine's Day in 1860. As 1856 drew to a close, Crawford's newspaper also announced the rebirth of an earlier society, the Washington Lyceum, devoted to learning and literature.[83]

Washington's growth during the first decade after Texas statehood did attract the notice of state political leaders. Gov. George T. Wood in 1848 appointed commissioners to pick a site for a state penitentiary. They visited Washington, anticipating that its location on the Brazos River might meet the transport requirements of the planned prison workshops, but ultimately the new operation was located in Huntsville, on the Trinity River. During April 1853, Washington D. Miller, Houston's erstwhile secretary and newspaper editor in Washington, staged a statewide convention of the Democratic Party in the former capital. Delegates came from just seven Texas counties, including journalist Joseph Lancaster and Mayor Henry R. Cartmell from Washington, and so the experiment was not repeated. In part the convention occurred because local Whigs had gathered at Washington in October 1852 to endorse Winfield Scott's presidential campaign. Whigs from the area met again during June 1853 to nominate candidates for governor and Congress, but that was the last time for Washington as the party faded nationwide.[84]

Local politicos were more successful in organizing a town government for Washington. The town incorporated again under state legislation on February 10, 1852. When elections were held in June 1853 for municipal officers, the main subject of discussion seemed to be the streets. Editor Lancaster declared that "our streets are a disgrace to a civilized community." Since 1851 a road overseer had tried to organize work days for "every citizen who has the prosperity of the place at heart" to gather at the ferry to "work the roads"

Robert A. Lott. *Courtesy of Star of the Republic Museum, Blinn College, Washington-on-the-Brazos State Historic Site, Washington, Texas.*

in Washington. Unfortunately for him and the community, he was usually ignored. The new city council in 1853 levied a tax on all property owners of six days per year to work on the roads, or they could pay three dollars in lieu of working. Again this apparently had no immediate effect: a stagecoach actually fell over as it made its way down the bluffs from Washington to the ferry in February 1854, prompting an angry outburst from Lancaster that local roads remained "disgraceful." George W. Crawford as the editor of the *Washington American* took up the charge in 1856, complaining that the city charter was just a "humbug" as local officials either passed laws they did not enforce or simply did nothing to improve the streets. He concluded that the city's charter ought to be repealed so streets could be improved under county road laws. There is no record of further improvements during the antebellum period.[85]

Another concern of local leaders such as Lancaster and Crawford was violent crime in Washington. George P. Lynch shot and killed a fellow Mason, Thomas B. Farrell, in June 1852, and he tried to kill Thomas P. Shapard. Washington Masonic Lodge No. 18 offered a reward of $100 for the capture of Lynch but withdrew the offer when the Grand Lodge declared that such an offer might attract negative attention. Crawford was one of a group of men who chased Lynch to Springfield, Texas, but there is no evidence that they caught him. G. W. McLees fired both loads from his double-barreled shotgun into E. J. Hendrick of Grimes County in April 1854. He claimed that Hendrick threatened his life, but he was arrested for murder and jailed in Brenham. When the court granted McLees a third continuance in October, he seized that opportunity to escape and flee the area. Such violence continued to be a problem in antebellum Washington. John Watson used a shotgun to kill W. V. Wright on a Washington street in August 1858. Since Watson was not jailed, he must have been more persuasive than McLees. At least one victim survived an attack in Washington: one of the Millican family of Brazos County had his thumb shot off in February 1860. Eight months later, former legislator Elliott M. Millican jumped to his death from a Washington hotel window after a bout of heavy drinking.[86]

White residents of Washington also worried about black violence, especially since slaves outnumbered free persons by 1860. Blacks were present in Washington from the start. John W. Hall, who owned twenty slaves, served as the first judge of the Washington municipality in 1836. One of the first cases over which he presided was the manumission of a black man and his wife, Andrew and Nancy, by James Walker. But there was a catch: they were not to be free until after both Walker and his wife died. Walker died in 1837; his wife, Catherine, lived until 1851, after Texas, like many Southern states, had adopted laws excluding free blacks except in very specific legal circumstances. Andrew James Walker and his wife Nancy eventually gained their freedom, but could not stay in Washington. They moved to the Rio Grande, where he drove a wagon at Eagle Pass and died shortly before the Civil War. There is no further record of what happened to Nancy. Thus everyone apparently got what they wanted, including those in Washington who considered an unfettered black man to be a threat. For them, proof surfaced when James Mitchell of Washington County and his cousin, Charles Donohoe, were allegedly severely beaten in 1852 by two of Mitchell's slaves.[87]

The Texas legislature gave the mayor of Washington the same authority in criminal and civil cases as a justice of the peace in an act signed on February 5, 1853. A little more than a year later, in August 1854, Robert A. Lott was elected mayor. A member of the Mier Expedition in 1842 who had survived by drawing a white bean in the Mexican decimation of prisoners, Lott operated a prominent hotel, just as his older brother, John A. Lott, had done during the era of the Republic of Texas. He and the city council established a patrol that summer to keep blacks from gathering in large groups in Washington, especially on Sundays. New laws required blacks away from their homes to have a pass, and thus it would be known if they were free or who should be responsible for them. Lancaster reported that the patrols quickly reduced the number of blacks "prowling about at all hours of the night" and the practice of large numbers of them gathering around the public square on Sundays. Some locals refused to serve on the patrols but changed their minds when Lott fined them. Patrols also confronted another practice that troubled whites: slaves hiring themselves to work and in other ways acting as if they were free. Lott chaired a hearing and ordered those who hired slaves to pay a fine or be jailed. Lancaster applauded this, remarking that blacks who were allowed to hire their own time usually became leaders in "deeds of rascality."[88]

By the fall of 1855, Washington had steamboats bringing cargo and hauling away cotton whenever the Brazos rose high enough to allow waterborne travel. The town's brick buildings housed all sorts of enterprises, including churches, schools, and an active town government. The community also had social organizations, including lodges or chapters of the Masons, Odd Fellows, and the Sons of Temperance. In other words, Washington at the close of its second decade of existence had many of the trappings of a commercially successful small southern town. A writer for the Austin *Texas State Gazette* remarked: "Upon the whole, Washington is a lively place with a thoroughly progressive and go-a-head population."[89] With such a strong start, people in Washington may well have believed their town would continue to prosper and even grow. But sadly for them, a turbulent decade of decline would soon end any pretensions to greatness.

Washington about 1860. *Courtesy of Star of the Republic Museum, Blinn College, Washington-on-the-Brazos State Historic Site, Washington, Texas.*

Chapter 4
ERA OF CONFLICT

Washington declined markedly from 1855 to 1865, as did many other communities in Texas and the nation as a whole. Economic stagnation and colossally bad business decisions created a tense atmosphere that enhanced angry political conflicts over the Union and slavery. The commitment of Washington leaders to steamboats as the vehicles for economic success, rather than railroads, led to the bypassing of the town as Texas developed a new commercial transportation network. But the effect of this decision was greatly enhanced by the Democratic Party's struggle to create a unified stand in defense of slavery against political challengers such as the American Party, which organized in Washington to launch a counterattack in Texas that stressed loyalty to the Union. This irreconcilable difference on the national stage drew Texans into the Civil War, greatly reducing the number of young men who could have been community leaders for the next generation. After a decade of such conflict, Washington no longer served as a significant center for economic or political activity.

After the mid-1850s, when there was a series of relatively dry years, only about a half dozen steamers traveled the Brazos River as far up as Washington. The finest among them was the *Fort Henry*, whose arrival during March 1855 was met with the firing of a cannon, cheering crowds, and a town meeting to thank the crew for coming at a time when water levels were low. In response, Capt. John H. King, an engineer who had previously operated a machine shop in Washington, hosted a party on board. Built at Wheeling, in what would become West Virginia, the steamboat was 153 feet long and 36 feet wide. Its 29 staterooms could accommodate 125 passengers, while another 116 rode as "deck" passengers. Reportedly it could float in sixteen inches of water when empty, and drew only thirty inches when loaded with eight hundred bales of cotton. It carried five hundred to six hundred bales when it left Washington in the spring of 1855 and was badly damaged by snags near Warren. King's partner, Capt. D. Verplanck Ackerman, brought the steamer back to Washington in the late summer and was stranded by low water. Stung by the loss of revenue, Ackerman took advantage of a wintertime flash flood and left in January 1856 with cotton and passengers, only to run aground in the canal between the Brazos River and Galveston. The steamboat was sold at auction in 1856 to settle debts, and ownership passed to Robert Mills. The *Fort Henry* made its last run on the Brazos in early 1858, when it landed at Washington on its way further upriver to Port Sullivan.[90]

The fate of two of the last steamboats to land at Washington illustrates just how fragile, and ultimately unreliable, such craft could be. The *Betty Powell*, a side-wheeler built on the Colorado River near La Grange for Samuel G. Powell of Galveston, arrived in March 1856. It carried three hundred bales of cotton on its downstream run, raising expectations for more successful operations as water levels remained low. Three years later it was destroyed in a fire. The last great hope of those in Washington who thought that steamboats would bring lasting prosperity appears to have been the *Belle Sulphur*. Pleasant B. Watson traveled on the steamer in the summer of 1858 as it traveled upriver from Washington to load cotton. About a dozen passengers were on board as an excursion, but the captain, whom Watson recalled as Henry R. Cartmell, drafted the young men to move bales. Built at New Albany, Indiana, in 1858, the steamer was constantly plagued with low water, but it carried hundreds of cotton bales to buyers downriver on several Brazos River runs. A Houston editor unkindly, but perhaps accurately, wrote, "She has much the appearance of an expensive plaything." He added, "If her owners have not paid dear for their whistle, we have been misinformed." The steamboat was lost in a storm in May 1862 while serving as a blockade runner.[91]

The continued bad luck of steamboats on the Brazos convinced many people that their economic future lay with railroads. The Buffalo Bayou, Brazos & Colorado Railroad Company was chartered in 1850 with the intent of linking Houston to the rich farms operating west of the port city. Thomas J. Heard, a versatile doctor who published an article on Washington that appeared in the *New Orleans Medical and Surgical Journal*, chaired a September 1853 meeting in town, with Wilson Y. McFarland (Sam Houston's host in 1843) as his secretary. The assembled townspeople heard an address by former Texas adjutant general Hugh McLeod on behalf of the Buffalo Bayou, Brazos & Colorado Railroad. Col. J. B. Ash of Galveston also urged support for the same enterprise in a Washington rally in April 1854. Unfortunately for Washington boosters, this line as it was built by 1855 ran from Houston to Richmond on the Brazos, far downstream from their town.[92]

Railroad supporters in Washington also lobbied for the Galveston and Red River Railroad Company. The first meeting on its behalf at Washington was in August 1853, when Henry R. Cartmell chaired a public gathering with George W. Crawford as his secretary. The president of the Galveston and Red River Railroad, Paul Bremond, spoke at length to the crowd, trying to sell subscriptions, or stock certificates. Apparently this scheme failed, but Bremond did not quit. Encouraged by Chappell Hill investors, he reorganized his company as the Houston and Texas Central Railway. Several times he and his agents tried to raise money by selling subscriptions at Washington, pointing out that this was the only way the rail line would cross the Brazos and run through that town, but each time they were rebuffed. The reason was obvious: as a correspondent wrote in the *Texas State Gazette,* "I have omitted to discuss at any length the idea of a railroad crossing the Brazos in Washington County because it is a notorious fact that the Washington county people have burned up their subscription books, and taken to navigating and cleaning out the Brazos river." Crawford told one meeting that if a subscription was not paid, "the time would come when Washington would be only a cotton patch and a memory." All such pleas fell on deaf ears, and the railroad reached Navasota just before the Civil War without crossing the Brazos.[93]

The completion of the Houston and Texas Central Railway to Navasota ended most steamboat traffic on the Brazos River by the eve of the Civil War. Much money had been spent to remove snags, dig a canal, and provide other improvements, but river trade still cost more and was less reliable than rail transport. The impact of this shift on Washington, where community leaders such as editor Joseph Lancaster and others had lobbied for the steamers, was evident. A Houston newspaper in 1858 reported that Washington "was once a flourishing town. Its citizens, however, do not bring good reports of its progress now." John S. Barton, who had come in time to witness the excitement of the riverboats arriving in Washington, was blunter in his memoir written many years later. He recalled that the community boomed "until the Texas Central, as a huge anaconda, strangled to the death both the town and its steamers."[94]

When it became clear that the Houston and Texas Central Railway was not going to cross the Brazos to the western bank where Washington lay, discussions began about building a line that would intersect "Bremond's Road." Crawford and others who promoted this idea understood that the state would give them land as reimbursement for the cost of construction. They even had a name for their firm: the Brazos Branch Railroad Company, chartered in 1854 and organized in 1857. The board included Crawford, D. M. Underhill, William P. Rogers, and other prominent local leaders and businessmen. They held a groundbreaking ceremony on the east bank of the Brazos, with Mayor Robert A. Lott and the directors each turning a shovelful of dirt. Debates intensified as the Houston and Texas Central approached Navasota. Editor W. J. Pendleton of the *Washington American* wrote that the real issue was whether Washington would soon become a "flourishing and prosperous Commercial and mercantile mart" or "an old, dilapidated worn-out-rat-eaten village." The tap road was never completed from Washington to Navasota.[95]

While Washington leaders discussed the construction of a rail line to link their town with Navasota, a rival road was being built to the south. The Washington County Rail Road Company was chartered by the legislature in February 1856 and began laying rails two years later. It was designed to connect Brenham with the Houston and Texas Central Railway at Hempstead by way of Chappell Hill. Tracks were placed on both sides of the Brazos by 1859, but it was early 1861 before a bridge, 260 feet long and sixty feet high, spanned the river. The war delayed new plans to link Washington with this new rail line, but in October 1866 the enabling legislation, actually an amendment of the original charter for the Brazos Branch Railroad Company, was approved. Again, nothing materialized from this initiative, perhaps because by that time the town had declined so much that its leaders could no longer muster the financial resources for such a costly project.[96]

While the steamboat trade on the Brazos River declined, and railroad supporters in Washington failed to have a link built to their town, the ferry originally established by Andrew Robinson in 1821 continued to operate. When his son-in-law John W. Hall enlisted others to help him develop the community, he reserved the ferry site for himself. He later sold it to his brother, Warren D. C. Hall, who in 1841 transferred it to his son and namesake. By 1853, the ferry was being operated by Thomas J. Heard and John Watson, who apparently were succeeded by C. Simonds during the fall of 1854 and by the partnership of Thomas H. Shepard and D. M. Underhill in early 1855. The latter two boasted that their ferry, built with local cedar, was the "largest, most convenient and complete ferry boat in the state." Seventy-eight feet long and twelve feet wide, it had "aprons" so that, when the river was low, wagons could use it as a bridge (and presumably still pay a toll). By the summer of 1856, only Underhill, who was also an investor in the Brazos Branch Railroad Company, still ran the ferry. It apparently continued to operate as the Civil War began but could hardly support significant commercial traffic.[97]

Washington community leaders during the years just before the Civil War debated their political future even more heatedly than their economic prospects. Texas Democrats faced a new challenge with the rise of the American Party, whose members were popularly called the "Know Nothings" because of their secrecy. The newcomers won local elections in Austin and Galveston in 1854, and then gathered in Washington for a state convention. They wooed voters with a platform that stressed nativism, Unionism, and states' rights, while they opposed any federal interference with slavery. They returned to Washington in June 1855 and met behind closed doors. Critics snarled that they were mostly former Whigs, and that Sam Houston, who lost his Senate seat when he refused to vote for the proslavery Kansas-Nebraska Act, was their leader. Any doubt about that dissipated when Houston published a letter supporting the Know Nothings, which prompted angry retorts from Anson Jones and Robert M. Williamson, who had represented Washington County in the Senate of the Republic of Texas. In July 1855

Satirical Sheet Music for the American Party. Prints & Photographs Division, Library of Congress. Washington, D. C.

the Know Nothings held a well-attended public rally in Washington, feeding the crowd barbecue and regaling them with a series of speeches. Local hero Robert E. B. Baylor, a judge and minister who helped found Baylor University, was elected as the Grand President of the Texas Know Nothings at this meeting.[98]

The Democratic counterattack began with the "Bombshell Convention" at Austin in June 1855. Williamson S. Oldham, who owned property in Washington, had attended the first Know Nothing meeting there, and then, after failing to secure a nomination for a public office, denounced the new party just days later at the Austin convention. As an editor of the *Texas State Gazette* he continued to condemn both the Know Nothings and Houston. Washington Democrats hosted their own caucus, chaired by Oldham, in late July, followed by a public rally and barbecue in August. Houston personally addressed the second gathering, hotly defending the Know Nothing ideals. Oldham followed with a speech that prompted a tirade from Houston that ended with the complete disruption of the meeting. The two men continued their exchange in a second forum held in the Methodist church at Washington one day later. The Democratic ticket, led by Elisha M. Pease as their candidate for governor, narrowly swept Washington County that month, but one of twelve Know Nothings elected to the legislature was John Sayles from Brenham, while Lemuel D. Evans, a former Whig who attended the Know Nothing caucus in Washington, was elected to the U.S. House of Representatives from Texas.[99]

After the August 1855 elections, the Know Nothings struggled to maintain their support in Washington as well as Texas. Prominent candidates, including Sayles, renounced their ties to the party. Henry Bailey, a Know Nothing serving as postmaster at Washington, was replaced with Calvin B. Ewing, a "sound reliable Democrat." When the American Party hosted a "Grand rally and ratification meeting" in Washington on the one-year anniversary of Houston's powerful speech, the speeches were given by local, not state, leaders such as Henry E. Lockett, who served as chief marshal for the parade that day. Disappointing results in the state and local elections in August 1856 led the Know Nothings in Washington to form a "Millard Fillmore for President" club, with Mayor Henry R. Cartmell in charge. They scheduled a "Grand Union Barbecue" in October 1856 that attracted a large crowd for the usual parade and even a speech by Houston, who refused to let a sudden downpour keep him from finishing his remarks. The victory of Democratic presidential candidate James Buchanan, who carried Washington County and Texas in the fall of 1856, sealed the fate of the Know Nothings in the state, and arguably left Unionists in Texas without a political focus at a crucial time.[100]

The Democrats triumphed in Washington and elsewhere in part because they claimed to be the true defenders of the Union. Thomas

J. Heard chaired a Democratic meeting during April 1856 at Washington that pledged support for the national party and its principles. This stand was seconded by prominent leaders who attended the caucus. Even more effective was Jones, who addressed a large crowd at Washington on July 29, 1856, expressing his strong support for the Union and his hope that it might be preserved. He drew a sharp contrast between his call for Texas independence in 1835 and his endorsement of the Union in 1856. Then, Texans faced a choice of annihilation or independence; twenty-one years later, they were prosperous and secure. As for the great concern of many Texans: "I will not insult this presence by presuming there is an Abolitionist within the sound of my voice; indeed, like certain reptiles that cannot breathe in a pure air, I do not suppose one could breathe the atmosphere of old Washington county and survive." But a "purely sectional" party had arisen, and "Black Republicanism," with its pledge to eradicate slavery through a plan given to them by British abolitionists, threatened the Union. Only the "great, national American Democratic Party," which followed the principles of George Washington, Thomas Jefferson, and Andrew Jackson, stood between the nation and ruin. Abolitionism and Black Republicanism had to be opposed, the Constitution sustained, and the Union preserved. Local Know Nothing leaders were present and delivered rebuttals, but few must have been listening.[101]

The battle between Know Nothings and Democrats created a sharp division between the two newspaper editors in Washington. Joseph Lancaster was a staunch Democrat who hated Know Nothings. The removal of Know Nothing Henry Bailey as the Washington postmaster prompted him to write: "the b'hoys raised one tremendous yell—guns were fired, bon-fires illuminated the town, and a general serenade pervaded Washington." When the Democrats carried Washington County in August 1855, he celebrated, under the headline "THE DEFEAT OF THE INVINCIBLE SAM," that "patriotic Democracy" had allied with "a few good old patriotic Whigs" to defeat Houston in his home county, despite the support of local leaders such as Baylor and the holding of a Know Nothing convention in Washington. He claimed that Know Nothings drove him out of Washington with a boycott in 1855, but his repeated complaints about deadbeat subscribers suggested that perhaps his real problem was a lack of revenue. He made a permanent move to Brenham during late 1856, but he continued to distribute his weekly paper in Washington, where he maintained his residence with Eva and their children.[102]

Crawford, who had joined the Know Nothings in 1854, just after completing a term as a member of the Texas House of Representatives, produced the first edition of the *Washington American* in November 1855 with the support of publisher George W. Perkins. Crawford's first publishing associate, Ewing, had been pro-Democrat and antislavery, and Wynne, with whom Crawford sometimes worked, was also a Democrat. By late 1855, however, Crawford opposed the Democrats and hated abolitionists. Perhaps to the relief of Lancaster, Crawford stayed with his new paper for only a year; he and Perkins sold their interests in the *Washington American* in November 1856 to W. J. Pendleton, who had been co-editing with Crawford for five months, and publisher R. B. Armfield. The last issue of the *Washington American* appeared on April 11, 1857.[103]

The primary point on which Democrats and Know Nothings appear to have agreed in antebellum Washington was the importance of slavery. Crawford and William P. Rogers, who left Washington in the late 1850s and later commanded a regiment for the Confederacy in the Civil War, played prominent roles in a "Kansas Meeting" at Robert A. Lott's Austin House hotel on June 19, 1856. The participants endorsed resolutions that had been adopted at an earlier meeting in nearby Independence that praised the proslavery Missouri Border Ruffians for their efforts to defeat the antislavery settlers in Kansas, and then joined with their colleagues in Independence in pledging to send money and men to support the fight against abolition in Kansas. The Washington meeting added its own warm praise for U.S. Rep. Preston Brooks of South Carolina, who had brutally beaten Sen. Charles Sumner of Massachusetts for his caustic remarks about those who supported slavery. A Fourth of July celebration at Washington just a few weeks later concluded with another rally for Kansas, with more angry resolutions adopted and more money raised to sustain the fight against those who sought to exclude slavery there.[104] There is no record that any men from Washington traveled to Kansas to fight for slavery, but town leaders certainly reacted when the threat of racial violence surfaced closer to home.

Fear of black insurrectionists erupted in Washington during the summer of 1856 when reports arrived of the discovery of a slave conspiracy in Colorado County. Allegedly a company of slaves had organized and prepared arms, intending to make their way to Mexico, by force if necessary. Editor Pendleton of the *Washington American* called for regular patrols to be re-established in Washington. Warming to his subject, a week later he declared that far too many blacks were being left unsupervised in Washington, often to hire their own time or buy alcohol. Alarmed residents gathered on September 18, 1856, for a "town meeting," at which they adopted resolutions that condemned the hiring of blacks and provided for the organization of a vigilance committee to devise effective methods of enforcement. The "Committee of General Vigilance and Safety" met for the first time two days later. The members declared an end to all "trading" with blacks and established a system of local patrols that operated under the direction of the committee, not the town government. The committee met again in late November, but when a black burglar was caught inside a Washington store, Pendleton and others demanded even more effective action.[105]

Robert A. Lott was then the mayor of Washington, and the events of 1856 sparked a strong reaction from him and his aldermen: Basil M. Hatfield, D. M. Underhill, B. F. Wilson, and Harden White. They adopted a series of ordinances in January 1857 that clearly addressed the complaints of many residents. Loud and unruly gatherings by both whites and blacks were banned. Fines would be levied on anyone who raced a horse through town, fired a gun in town, or was drunk in public. Saloons, pool halls, and bowling alleys would be fined if not closed on Sunday. Any black found in town without written permission from his or her owner would automatically receive thirty-nine lashes. Fines would be levied on anyone who sold liquor to a slave without the written permission of his or her owner. Any black who bought or rented a building in Washington would be whipped, and his or her owner would be fined. Patrols under city supervision would be established to enforce the new laws. A long list of municipal taxes would be assessed, and the revenues would be spent on law enforcement and improving the streets.[106]

Lott's measures did not address all local concerns, but he did seem to focus on the most important issues: controlling lawlessness, especially by blacks, in a time of growing conflict, and trying to encourage commerce by keeping the streets passable. Washington seems to have had a problem with stray hogs, which appeared to be unstoppable in their constant quest for something to eat. The new laws said nothing about that. There was also no provision for a fire company, a recurring complaint in the newspapers. Lancaster was particularly anxious about fire because he lost his office in November 1852 when a candle was left burning inside. The same conflagration consumed the saddle shop and residence of Henry R. Cartmell, as well as several other buildings. But there was only so much money in Washington in the best of times, and Lott's efforts to levy taxes for law enforcement and street improvements came at a time when the town was clearly stagnating. A visitor in 1859 reported that Washington had "a large number of well constructed business houses, but unfortunately, the builders reckoned without their host, for most of the houses are now unoccupied for the want of tenants." While a "tolerable brisk business" was being conducted, it was clear that it was only a fraction of what it had been.[107]

Washington did contribute some manpower to the fight for slavery on another front. Crawford left the *Washington American* in late 1856 to lead a company of Texans to join the forces of William Walker in Nicaragua. Walker had declared himself president of Nicaragua in July 1856 with the support of both American filibusters and Nicaraguan allies. He then attracted even greater support in the southern United States by reinstating slavery. By the fall of 1856 he was besieged in his capital city of Granada by a Central American coalition army that greatly outnumbered his forces. Many Southerners responded. Crawford, in November 1856, called for a "Nicaragua meeting" at Lott's hotel, which had hosted a rally for Kansas just five months earlier. He intended to muster a company on November 19 and leave the next day for the war. He declared in the *Washington American* that this was a great opportunity to expand slavery, as slaves could be used to produce coffee and sugar in Nicaragua, and get rich, as many confiscated estates would be sold. He added that all of his recruits would be provided with horses, weapons, and equipment.[108]

Crawford and his recruits actually left Washington on the stagecoach on the night of November 18, 1856. There were just three men with Crawford: Pleasant B. Watson, a young man who had played a prominent role in Know Nothing rallies alongside Crawford, and two other fellows identified only as D. Burnett and D. M. Smith. At New Orleans, Crawford continued to call for recruits, conveying the information through the *Washington American* that all volunteers would get free passage to Nicaragua, 250 acres, and $25 per month in pay. Watson recalled that "a good many" enlisted, but there were no others from Washington. Crawford left New Orleans for Nicaragua as the captain of a small company of Texans and arrived near Granada on January 7, 1857. Five days later he led his men, and others, in an attack on the forces besieging Granada. After hard fighting, during which Crawford led three assaults, the attackers broke through and rescued their comrades, who retreated to the coast after burning the city. Crawford was wounded in the arm, so Walker promoted him to colonel and sent him home to recruit. Watson came with him, but the fates of Burnett and Smith are unknown.[109]

Crawford may have left Washington almost alone and at night, but he returned a hero. The editors of two Texas newspapers had been remarkably unkind in their comments about his departure, focusing on the irony of an anti-Catholic nativist who had refused to go to Kansas to fight for slavery suddenly deciding to battle for the same institution in Nicaragua. But Pendleton had staunchly defended his colleague, writing that since Walker had declared slavery legal "the unwavering finger of destiny points out to the South its true course." After reports of Crawford's military exploits surfaced, the Austin *Texas State Gazette* was gracious enough to declare that he "behaved well and gallantly" and "well deserved" a promotion. Pendleton gloated that his fellow editor was now the "Hero of Granada," returning home "crowned with the laurels of his highest hopes." Crawford and his men, according to Pendleton, charged 1,600 enemy troops and rescued 150 Americans. Much of Pendleton's information came from Crawford himself, who arrived in Washington by February 1857. A "Nicaragua Ball" was held at Lott's hotel, where speeches were made and resolutions were adopted that praised Crawford and condemned the federal government for opposing Walker. Crawford again traveled to Houston by March 1857 to recruit, allegedly gathering as many as 240 volunteers. Plans were announced to expand his command to two companies, and Pendleton claimed that Crawford would take charge of all Texans with Walker when he returned to Nicaragua.[110]

News of the defeat of Walker, who returned to the United States by the summer of 1857, persuaded Crawford to quit his military plans, but not politics. He again settled in Washington and campaigned unsuccessfully for the Texas Senate. Although the Democratic ticket led by gubernatorial candidate Hardin R. Runnels swept Washington County in 1857, opposition to them remained strong. Houston once more spoke at a barbecue in Washington in the summer of 1858, and Crawford campaigned on his behalf during his successful bid for the governor's office in 1859. In return, Houston appointed Crawford as the brigadier general in charge of the militia district that included Washington. Crawford did not return to journalism, perhaps because of the commercial decline of Washington. Lancaster stayed in Brenham, while two other men tried and failed to start papers in Washington in the late 1850s: James H. Littlefield in early 1857 with the *Washington Democrat*, and then John A. Moore during early 1858 with the *Washington National Register*.[111]

The economic and political arguments in Washington during the 1850s proved to be a prelude to an even more tragic conflict. The 1860 presidential campaign bitterly divided the town and the country. But this time the leading players changed. Crawford, who as a staunch Know Nothing had hotly opposed the Democrats, delivered a speech at Lott's hotel in September 1860 in which he strongly endorsed the Democratic ticket of John C. Breckinridge and Joseph Lane for president and vice president respectively. He declared that he still supported the Union, but if Abraham Lincoln and the other Republicans treated the South unfairly, then he would have to endorse disunion. Crawford consistently promoted the "Breckinridge and Lane Club," which held a "Grand rally" at Washington in late September 1860. At the same time, Unionists held a gathering in Washington, at which Crawford spoke in opposition to his old Know Nothing ally Henry E. Lockett. They also planned a barbecue for October 1860, at which Constitutional Union Party electors George W. Paschal and Andrew J. Hamilton would speak. Hamilton, a U.S. congressman, was actually blocked from speaking at that event until Williamson S. Oldham, who had

Jerome B. Robertson. *Historical Research Center, Texas Heritage Museum, Hill College, Hillsboro, Texas.*

recently moved from Austin to Brenham, intervened, demanding that he be allowed to talk. Hamilton did so, but afterwards he was told not to speak again in Washington County, a warning that he apparently heeded.[112]

The election of Lincoln as president galvanized many in the Gulf South, which included Texas, into supporting secession. Hundreds of men attended a meeting at Brenham in December 1860. Crawford served on the steering committee, which adopted resolutions endorsing disunion and nominated three men to serve as delegates to the impending Secession Convention in Austin: Oldham, Jerome B. Robertson, and James E. Shepard. The latter two were with Crawford on the steering committee. Robertson lived at Independence but had originally settled at Washington, where he was mayor in 1839–1840 and later served as postmaster. Shepard, like Robertson, had been in the Texas legislature after moving to Brenham in 1846. All three men supported leaving the Union as delegates to the Secession Convention and became ardent Confederates, Oldham as a senator in the Confederate Congress, Robertson as the colonel of the Fifth Texas Infantry and later a brigadier general, and Shepard as the lieutenant colonel of the Sixteenth Texas Infantry. Interestingly, Robertson's son Felix H. Robertson, born at Washington in 1839, also became a Confederate brigadier general.[113]

Before the voters of Texas endorsed the secession ordinance in a popular referendum in February 1861, in which Washington County voted in favor of disunion, a militia company had already formed in Washington. Dr. John D. Rogers, a graduate of Tulane University practicing medicine in Washington, organized and became the captain of the Dixie Blues, which mustered as Company E of the Fifth Texas Infantry in the brigade later commanded by John Bell Hood in the Army of Northern Virginia. Rogers had attended the school directed by Lindsay P. Rucker, and he served as one of the secretaries for the secession caucus at Brenham in December 1860, but he had no military experience. Fortunately for him and his men, Robertson, who took charge of their regiment and then the brigade in 1862, had commanded volunteers in campaigns against Indians in 1838 and Mexicans in 1842, during the Somervell Expedition.[114]

The Dixie Blues, with Rogers as captain, arrived in Virginia after the first Battle of Bull Run and settled on the Potomac River to watch for the enemy. Sickness swept the Texas camp, but Rogers's

Flag of the 5th Texas Infantry, CSA. *Courtesy of Texas State Library and Archives Commission.*

company had only eighteen men in the hospital at Dumfries in the fall of 1861, far fewer than many companies in their brigade. Robertson took command of the Fifth Texas Infantry in time for their first real battle in June 1862 at Gaines's Mill, where the Dixie Blues mustered fifty-two officers and men. The Fifth Texas captured two Union regiments but the Dixie Blues had at least three men killed and eleven wounded, or more than one-fourth of their number. At least one private, Rufus K. Felder of Chappell Hill, reported that casualties in the company totaled nineteen. Among the wounded was Lt. Walter N. Norwood, whose father, Nathaniel Norwood, came to Washington during the Republic period to operate a public house. A bullet struck him in the chest and was only stopped by the Bible he carried in his pocket. Another member of the Dixie Blues was killed and two wounded at Malvern Hill in early July, when the retreating Union army made a stand and bloodied the Army of Northern Virginia.[115]

Rufus K. Felder and Miers M. Felder. *Historical Research Center, Texas Heritage Museum, Hill College, Hillsboro, Texas.*

Rogers left Company E after Malvern Hill, having been given permission to raise a regiment back home in Texas. Felder remarked that the men did not miss him, as he was not an attentive commander. Thomas A. Baber was promoted from lieutenant to captain in his place and led the Dixie Blues at the second Battle of Bull Run, where Robertson again commanded the regiment. The Fifth Texas won fame for crushing the Fifth New York Infantry in a furious charge that drove the Federals back for several miles and left the battlefield littered with their dead and wounded, but the Dixie Blues again paid heavily for their success. Of the sixty-three officers and men in the fight, three were killed and seventeen wounded; among the latter, five later died. Pleasant B. Watson was among the wounded men who survived. He had joined the Dixie Blues in time for the battle at Gaines's Mill and was wounded by a shell fragment at Second Bull Run. Lieutenant Norwood dressed his wound and put him on a horse for a ride to the hospital, whence he returned to Texas that fall. Watson agreed with Felder in again reporting higher losses, twenty-five killed and wounded of forty men in the battle, although Felder also claimed that the Fifth Texas suffered more casualties than any other Confederate regiment at Second Bull Run.[116]

Having defeated two Union armies, the Army of Northern Virginia invaded Maryland, seeking the decisive victory that might end the war. Robertson, wounded in the shoulder at Gaines's Mill and in the groin at Second Bull Run, had to relinquish command of his regiment to the next-highest-ranking officer who remained in the field: Capt. Ike N. M. Turner. Only thirty-eight officers and men from the Dixie Blues fought in the cornfield at Antietam in mid-September 1862, when the Union forces fumbled an opportunity to trap the Confederates. The company suffered relatively light losses: Baber and Norwood were wounded, along with three privates, while three others were killed or died of their wounds. This paled in comparison to the casualties suffered by the First Texas Infantry, which reported that more than 80 percent of its complement had been killed or wounded that day.[117]

Robertson recovered from his wounds and took command of the brigade after Antietam, when Hood was promoted to lead a division. The next trial by fire came at Gettysburg, where the brigade suffered six hundred casualties, of which one-third were in the Fifth

Walter N. Norwood. *Historical Research Center, Texas Heritage Museum, Hill College, Hillsboro, Texas.*

Texas Infantry. Robertson was once more wounded, while Robert M. Powell, who had been promoted to colonel of the Fifth Texas, was wounded and captured. Baber led an unknown number of the Dixie Blues into the Devil's Den at the base of the Round Tops, where most of the fighting took place for the Texans. Four men from the company were killed, while another eleven were wounded, of whom six became prisoners like their colonel, and three later died. Shuttled just months later to northern Georgia, the brigade made a decisive charge at Chickamauga, where Baber reported eleven casualties, two killed and nine wounded. There were very few Dixie Blues left to bid Robertson farewell in early 1864 when he clashed with his corps commander, Lt. Gen. James Longstreet. Relieved of his brigade command, Robertson was ordered to Texas on recruiting duty.[118]

Baber also returned home on recruiting duty in early 1864, so Lt. Bolling Eldridge led the Dixie Blues in the horrific fighting of the Wilderness Campaign. On May 5, 1864, the brigade rushed to the front about sunrise, confronting a surprise Union attack. Gen. Robert E. Lee rode to meet them, asking the identity of the welcome reinforcements. Their new commander, Brig. Gen. John Gregg of Texas, proudly responded that they were the Texas Brigade, prompting Lee to declare that he could always depend on the men from the Lone Star State to drive the enemy. When Lee suddenly turned to lead the counterattack, Leonard G. Gee of the Dixie Blues grabbed Traveller's bridle as his colleagues loudly declared that they would not advance until the army commander retired to safety. Records indicate that two-thirds of the Fifth Texas Infantry fell in the successful assault. Among these casualties were two men killed and seven wounded in the Dixie Blues. Lt. Thomas Nash, who had been wounded at Gaines's Mill and the second Battle of Bull Run, was among the dead. The wounded included Eldridge and Gee.[119]

Pvt. Rufus K. Felder wrote home after Cold Harbor, where the Dixie Blues participated in a slaughter of the Union troops and had only one of their number wounded, that he and his comrades were "in fine spirits." But in fact the Army of Northern Virginia was forced into the trenches in front of Petersburg, where constant fighting with the larger Union forces gradually reduced the Confederates. Three members of the Dixie Blues were wounded in fighting along the siege lines, while another three were wounded in a sally at Darbytown Heights, where they encountered Federals with repeating carbines for the first time. One of the wounded was Baber, who had returned to his command from Texas. It is difficult to say how many men served in the Dixie Blues during the war. Watson for example does not appear in company muster rolls, but it does appear that the fifteen who signed paroles at Appomattox represented about 10 percent of the total, with 90 percent killed, wounded, captured, or otherwise absent.[120]

What happened to the Dixie Blues who came home during the

war is an interesting question, but only a few stories are known. A. J. Stevens, originally a sergeant and then a lieutenant in the company, returned to Texas on a recruiting trip in 1862 but was back in Virginia, working as a nurse in a Richmond hospital, in 1863. The next year he was sent to the Trans-Mississippi region on a "secret service" assignment, but he campaigned to be the sheriff of Washington County during the summer of 1864. Pleasant B. Watson recovered from his wound and during April 1864 raised a company and joined Col. Santos Benavides's regiment at Laredo. When John S. "Rip" Ford approached with his Rio Grande Expeditionary Force, Watson and his men accompanied Capt. José del Refugio Benavides to join Ford. After one brief skirmish and the subsequent occupation of Brownsville, Watson with his company was detailed to establish a trade route to the King Ranch and establish posts to guard it. He was among the troopers sent in late 1864 to attack Brazos Santiago, but a winter storm delayed the attack and the Federals, realizing the threat, shifted to meet the Confederates. Watson saw one of his own men shot dead while standing next to him. The bitter cold made him sick, so he left for home, but he met his family in Houston, where he held his daughter, born in October 1864, for the first time.[121]

Soldiers such as Watson had little choice about re-entering the service after 1862. That year the embattled Confederacy, struggling to fill the ranks of its armies, enacted the first draft in American history. When the war began, Crawford was the brigadier general for the local militia district, appointed by Gov. Sam Houston. When reports circulated that evacuating Federals had taken control of the port of Indianola during April 1861, Crawford gathered men at Washington to meet the threat. Fortunately for them, this rumor proved false. By early 1862, John Sayles succeeded Crawford as commander of the reorganized Twenty-Third Militia District, and he clashed with Confederate and state officials over the drafting of men who enrolled in his militia companies. James P. Flewellen, a West Point graduate who bought Barrington in 1858 to settle near his brother Robert T. Flewellen, who served in the Texas House of Representatives from 1859 to 1863, replaced John S. "Rip" Ford as the state commandant of conscription in late 1862. Flewellen lasted only a few months as commandant before Ford was reappointed in his place to work more closely with Confederate authorities. Sayles had to lead several of his companies, mustered as the Fourth Regiment of Texas State Troops, in September 1863 to Hempstead, where they guarded prisoners at Camp Groce. By that time, Sayles had sent more than five hundred men into the Confederate armies, but the bottomlands along the Brazos were reputed to be full of shirkers and deserters. Joseph Lancaster, as a captain for the Confederacy, was assigned in April 1864 to enforce the draft in the Brazos region during the last year of the war.[122]

Conscription brought men into the Confederate armies, while new war taxes and even impressments provided them with the arms and supplies that they badly needed. Col. George W. White, the commissary agent for the Confederacy in Texas, drew criticism for his heavy-handed administration of impressment policies. A meeting of the officers of the Third Cavalry Battalion, Texas State Troops, which included a company from Washington County led by Capt. James L. Dallas of Brenham, adopted an angry resolution in early 1864 which declared that if any person continued to confiscate goods, "we will suspend him to the nearest black jack limb to the place where he may be caught." At the same time, they pledged that the same would be done to any "shirker" who stole from local families, especially any active soldier's family. The officers did pledge to defend Texas from any invaders, and to give one-tenth of their annual production to support the Confederacy, but they resented the desperate measures taken to sustain the Southern war effort. Dallas had actually served as sheriff of Washington County prior to the war, but he apparently joined with his subordinates in their extralegal threats.[123]

On the home front in Washington, women often emerged as heroes in their attempts to keep businesses open and support the soldiers. Lancaster's wife, Eva, published their newspaper after he and their two sons departed for Confederate service. Their younger son, William W., was just fourteen years of age when he enlisted in the Twenty-Fourth Texas Cavalry in March 1862; he left the service after about eight months and came home to help his mother with the newspaper. Francis B., or Frank, was eighteen when he joined the Second Texas Cavalry in September 1861. He came home on leave in late 1863 to assist his mother and remained almost a year before returning to his regiment. Eva may not have needed much help. She was active in raising "hospital funds" for soldiers with "benefit concerts, fairs, etc." The officers of the Second Texas Cavalry in February 1863 sent their thanks to her and the "Ladies of the Washington Female Collegiate Institute," as well as the rest of the residents of Washington, for sending $540.10 raised through a concert and presentation. A "Concert and Tableaux" held at Washington in March 1863, along with a ball and supper, generated $786.50 for the Texas Brigade in Virginia. Eight prominent Washington ladies, led by Eva Lancaster and Mary Cartmell, published an emotional appeal for an event to support the Texas soldiers serving in Arkansas, where Lancaster's younger son had been posted. Despite the costs of elaborate staging such as "Chemicals for Red Fire" and the services of a band, the public concert and theatrical production they presented at Washington in April yielded a profit of $1,203.50, which Eva sent to the troops.[124]

The disruptions of the war years had a clear impact on Washington. Sarah Johnson wrote to a friend in November 1864 that her town had become a "perfect wreck," with many residences "pulled down and removed." Apparently many provided materials to build new homes in nearby Navasota. At the same time, "all of the large brick stores" were "filled with tithe corn," sent by farmers to pay war taxes or fulfill impressment directives. Plans had been laid for establishing a military depot in December 1863; Ruter Chapel, which had been abandoned after it developed structural cracks, was used to store military supplies until its roof collapsed. Independence Hall, which had been used for many purposes since hosting the Convention in March 1836, reportedly burned during this period. All of this must have greatly complicated the efforts of Benjamin F. Rucker, a longtime druggist in Washington who served as the Washington County agent for the distribution of relief funds to the families of men in Confederate service. On the other hand, C. P. Monroe, an enterprising young blacksmith, began buying empty land at this time, and within twenty years he owned most of the townsite.[125]

Despite the hard times, schools and churches did not disappear entirely. The Methodists struggled, but other denominations fared better. The Baptists held a well-attended revival in their church during the summer of 1864 and baptized eleven people, including Joseph Lancaster. The Presbyterian Synod of Texas convened at Washington during November 1864. While student numbers, espe-

Benjamin F. Rucker's Store. *Courtesy of Star of the Republic Museum, Blinn College, Washington-on-the-Brazos State Historic Site, Washington, Texas.*

cially of males, dropped, as did the amount of state money spent on education, the Reverend Robert S. Seeley of St. Paul's Episcopal Church continued to operate his Female Academy. Seeley also served as the postmaster of Washington, taking the place of Calvin B. Ewing in 1864 and serving until after the war ended. The Washington Female Collegiate Institute also remained open, at least until 1863.[126]

Despite their valiant efforts, individuals and small groups could not undo the damage done to Washington by a decade of economic, political, and military conflict. Having failed to link into the railroad network in Texas, Washington by 1865 was no longer a commercial center of any importance. Many of the leaders who might have corrected this mistake had been lost in a bloody national conflict after committing themselves to a military defense of slavery rather than the Union. Having already lost the prominence of being a seat of government, Washington after the Civil War faced a bleak future with little prospect of regaining any of its former commercial vigor.

Chapter 5

SHADOW TOWN

Washington during and immediately after the Reconstruction era became an arena for battles between white Democrats and black Republicans for control of county politics, prompting some residents to leave while others struggled unsuccessfully to revive the town's commercial past. While Washington County's population grew by about half from 1865 to 1900, the town of Washington lost its government and shrank to a community of about one hundred people, a mere shadow of its antebellum self. At the same time, it began to shift from an Anglo community to one dominated by Germans as the proportion of foreign-born residents in Washington County rose exponentially.[127] But this was not the only demographic transition the town experienced. Located in a precinct with an already substantial black population, Washington increasingly became a black community during the third and fourth decades of the twentieth century. After World War II, Washington almost vanished, but then the county's shrinking populace was reshaped by an influx of wealthy outsiders who were attracted by the natural beauty of the area. Fortunately for Washington, they proved to be interested in preserving the history of the region.

Conflict before and during the Civil War greatly reduced Washington, and then the era of Reconstruction brought new trouble. Much of that initially focused on the family of Pleasant B. Watson. In June 1865, Pleasant and his brother John, with their wives and daughters (one each), decided to leave Washington and move west rather than live under Yankee domination. Pleasant had married Eugenia Cartmell, daughter of former mayor Henry R. Cartmell and his wife, Mary, so his wife's brother James Cartmell decided to go with them. The group left on June 12, taking with them four slaves, two boys and two girls. At San Marcos, the two boys disappeared with a pair of the Watson's mules and their saddles. After a series of such misfortunes, which included becoming very ill, Pleasant decided the frontier was not for him. He and his brother John returned to Washington with their families, which proved to be an even more unfortunate decision for them.[128]

President Andrew Johnson allowed the defeated Confederate states to rebuild their own governments, which led to a restoration of Democratic power in the hands of ex-Confederates throughout the South, including Texas. Republicans in Congress responded in early 1867 with the Reconstruction Acts, which placed most southern states in a military district. Texas was in the Fifth Military District, and military officials there provided for a new registration of loyal voters during April 1867. Three registrars were appointed for Washington County: Peter Diller, Louis E. Edwards, and Benjamin O. Watrous. Diller was a Unionist merchant from Pennsylvania who fled Texas during the war but returned afterward and became a Republican. Edwards came to Brenham with the Union army and remained after he was discharged. Watrous was a former slave born in Tennessee who had already established a church and a school in Brenham. Elected to the state constitutional convention in 1868 as a Republican, he was one of five black delegates who signed the new state constitution. Obviously they were not the sort of people who would be welcomed by ex-Confederates such as the Watsons.[129]

The trio began registering voters in Washington County during the summer of 1867, meeting with an especially positive reaction from the black majority that lived there. This may have contributed to their confrontation at Washington with John Watson, Felix Farquhar, and John W. Gee. Watson was forty-five years of age at about the time conscription was enacted, so he was exempt and apparently never volunteered. Farquhar, who was married to Watson's half-sister Mary Autry, had served in the Dixie Blues with Pleasant Watson; he returned home after he was wounded at Gettysburg, but his brother Cornelius E. Farquhar had remained with the Dixie Blues until he was killed in the Wilderness. Gee was the brother of Leonard G. Gee, who had grabbed Traveller's bridle at the Wilderness to stop Gen. Robert E. Lee from leading the Texans' charge. John Gee served with his brother in the Dixie Blues until he was wounded at the second Battle of Bull Run, after which he trans-ferred to a cavalry unit. All three were dangerous: Watson used a shotgun to kill a man, W. V. Wright, on a Washington street in August 1858; Farquhar was free on bail after he slashed H. Menan, a Jewish merchant, with his knife; and Gee had already shot and killed a man named J. Bramlet in Brazos County.[130]

In July 1867, Watson, Farquhar, and Gee came to Washington; allegedly Farquhar had not yet secured his bail money or an attor-ney after his arrest for cutting Menan, so that was the reason he was in town. Spotting two of the federal registrars, Edwards and Watrous, the three, with a drunken Gee in the lead, confronted them. Words may or may not have been exchanged, but Gee sud-denly shot both of them. When James G. Hurd, a Texas Navy vet-eran then serving as a municipal court judge in Galveston, tried to intervene, Watson held his shotgun on him so Gee could ride away. Watson then tried to shoot Edwards, but he was restrained by the crowd, and soldiers arrived to take him and Farquhar into custody. The two prisoners were taken to Brenham and then transferred to Houston, but Gee remained free, which prompted a meeting of citi-zens at Washington to offer a reward for his capture. Fortunately, the wounds suffered by the registrars proved to be slight, and they soon recovered.[131]

Pleasant Watson of course believed that his relatives were "per-fectly innocent," and he got many witnesses to sign a petition attesting to that fact, which he sent to federal authorities. The two prisoners were brought before a military commission in August 1867, but no verdict was reached and they stayed in prison until they escaped a few weeks later. John Watson and Farquhar then returned to Washington, where they received a letter from Capt. Edward Collins, commander of the Federal troops at Brenham, telling them that if they would come to him, he would give them paroles. They went to Brenham in November 1867 along with Ban-nister "Ban" Wells Farquhar, Felix's younger brother, and Thomas "Tommie" Autry, the Watsons' half-brother. Felix and Tommie waited in a hotel lobby, while John and Ban were elsewhere. A detachment of Federal soldiers, under Lt. William H. H. Crowell, surrounded the hotel; some of the soldiers then entered and shot Felix in the chest and Tommie in the neck. Felix, who at least one witness claimed was drawing his weapon when he was shot, died instantly; Tommie, who was only seventeen years of age, died a few days later.[132]

The Federals later claimed that killing Felix and Tommie was a mistake; they were in fact looking for John Gee. Pleasant Watson angrily recalled: "I couldn't get 10 good men to go with me to attack them [the Federals at Brenham]. I tried to have them tried by law for it but couldn't succeed. I hope that Hevens Vengeance may fall heavily upon the murderers." Bitter, he left Washington and moved with his family to Houston. Gee was never arrested; in 1909 he donated two dollars for the Hood's Texas Brigade monument, which was dedicated the following year on the grounds of the Texas Capitol. At the time, he lived openly in Bryan, using his own name. Ban Farquhar was shot dead in 1879 by a neighbor, John Monroe, after a longstanding feud. No definite evidence concerning the fate of John Watson has been found.[133]

Reconstruction violence at Washington actually compelled at least one prominent Democrat to become a Republican. Joseph Lancaster moved to Navasota during the Civil War and began publishing his newspaper there. In July 1868, his younger son, William, was traveling through Washington County and decided to spend the night with a former slave of the Lancaster family. Three disguised white vigilantes took William from the house where he was staying and lynched him. Andrew Holliday was indicted for the murder of William Lancaster in September 1868, but no further record of a trial has been found. It may be that William's death is linked to the incident known as the Millican Riot, which erupted at about the same time as his murder when reports emerged in that Brazos County community that Holliday had lynched a popular black leader named Miles Brown. A black militia company that mustered to arrest Holliday clashed violently with white volunteers, leaving at least six blacks dead. Brown had not been killed by Holliday but instead had fled to Washington County. Holliday thus did not murder Brown, but garbled reports of William Lancaster's death may have sparked the violence in Millican. Regardless, Joseph Lancaster was furious about his son's murder and felt betrayed by the white Democrats who did nothing to avenge him. A stalwart Democrat up to that point in his life, he became a Republican and moved his newspaper to Austin, where he was supported by Gov. Edmund J. Davis. His older son, Frank, a Confederate veteran like William, joined the State Police, reviled by Democrats as agents of Republican oppression, in 1871.[134]

The determination of Democrats to reduce black political power in Washington County kept the area in turmoil even after the Reconstruction era. Thousands of blacks joined the Union League, organized with Watrous as leader, and this formed the basis for the Republican Party in the county. A few white Unionists and former Whigs joined them, as well as a growing number of German immigrants. There were just over 1,000 Germans in Washington County in 1860, but this number grew to about 3,500 by 1890, when one-fourth of the county's residents could claim German ancestry. After the Civil War, as large plantations in the county were sold or leased in parcels by their owners, Germans came to Washington County to acquire land. The county clerk reported in March 1866 that Germans had bought ninety parcels, totaling 10,800 acres, during the past six months. While this initially brought more votes to the black-dominated Republican Party in Washington County, ultimately white Republicans were not inclined to stand with their black allies against a determined conservative white Democratic counterattack, especially one that sought to control the ballot box through violence.[135]

Democrats regained control of state-level politics in Texas by the mid-1870s, thereby bringing an effective end to Reconstruction, but black political strength persisted in Washington County with blacks, or whites they supported, holding county offices and seats in the legislature. This was especially true in the two eastern precincts, in which Chappell Hill and Washington were located. Both precincts were overwhelmingly black, which attracted violent opposition. Initially blacks were killed by "disguised men in the night" throughout Washington County during the years immediately after the Civil War. By 1878, Republicanism had faded in many parts of the county, but not everywhere. A writer for the *Brenham Weekly Banner* that summer noted there was a large Juneteenth celebration at Washington, but he took solace in a report from a visitor who claimed that two hundred white voters had recently settled there. He concluded, "This precinct was formerly as dark as Erebus, but the advent of these white voters will shed a ray of light on the precinct that will absolutely astonish the managers of the Senegambian ring." Such confidence faded after a caucus at Washington pledged

Washington about 1870. *Courtesy of Star of the Republic Museum, Blinn College, Washington-on-the-Brazos State Historic Site, Washington, Texas.*

350 black votes to support a "black and tan" Republican coalition. The ballots cast at Washington in November strongly rejected the Democratic ticket, from the governor down, and contributed to the countywide defeat of every Democratic candidate but one for state offices. Six blacks were elected to the Texas legislature in 1878, two of whom were from Washington County: Bedford G. Guy from William Penn, near Washington, and Alonzo Sledge from Chappell Hill.[136]

The showdown came in 1886, after the Democrats in Washington County spent eight more years trying to use racism to recruit Germans and other whites from the Republican Party and again resorting to violence. The November contest was between the remaining Republicans and a "People's Party" alliance of Democrats and a few white Republicans. Three black election officials had been killed at Chappell Hill in 1884, so in 1886 the election judge there, a member of the People's Party, kept his polls closed. The precinct in which Washington lay thus became the main battleground. On the afternoon of November 2, 1886, County Judge Lafayette Kirk telegraphed D. D. Bolton, a candidate for county commissioner on the People's Party ticket with Kirk, asking him to intervene with the ballots being cast at the estate of Robert T. Flewellen, who had actually moved to Houston several years earlier. Kirk visited the polling place and found that a black Republican had indeed defeated the People's Party candidate for county clerk there. He left after speaking with the election judge. About sundown, three armed white men wearing masks entered the polling station. Polk Hill, a sharecropper, fired his shotgun into the face of the first intruder, DeWees Bolton, D. D. Bolton's son, killing him instantly. Everyone immediately fled, leaving the dead man to be found the next morning. Two other black-majority communities near Washington were also targeted. Ballots from Lott's Store, where the Republicans had also won, were given to C. P. Spann and Marshall Booker for transport to Brenham on November 2, but they were robbed near Independence by three more armed men. At Graball, where again Republicans had won, the ballots were destroyed by another trio of armed, masked white men.[137]

The affair escalated in the days following the fight for the ballot boxes. In response to Kirk's claims that a black uprising was imminent, militia went to Flewellen's place and Graball on November 8, 1886, but they found nothing. Eight black men were arrested the following day for the killing of Bolton and taken to Houston. They were later transferred to Brenham, where on the night of December 2 vigilantes took three of the eight from the county jail and lynched them. The other five prisoners were released on bail and never brought to trial. The federal district attorney in Austin filed charges against Kirk and others for the events at Flewellen's place, Lott's Store, and Graball. Kirk's defense attorneys, who served without pay, were former governor John Ireland, former U.S. representative John Hancock, former Texas state senator Seth Shepard of Washington County, chairman William W. Searcy of the Washington County Democratic executive committee, and incumbent U.S. senator Richard Coke. Senator Coke sat with Kirk during his August 1887 trial, which ended in an acquittal from the white Democratic jury.[138]

Petitions from leading Republicans, who were outraged at losing Washington County in such a manner, soon led to a congressional investigation of the election-day violence in the first precinct of Washington County. Senator Coke led the opposition to the petitioners in early 1888 before the U.S. Senate, along with Ireland.

Kirk and his colleagues, including Bolton, testified on their own behalf, claiming that they had acted to prevent an uprising among the blacks. One of the Washington County Republicans asked to speak was Robert J. Moore, a black resident of Graball who told the Senate that he lived in Washington. Moore had defeated a black challenger in 1878 to retain his seat as a county commissioner, and since that time he had served several terms in the legislature. He probably understood how the political climate was changing, so his answers to most of the senators' questions were noncommittal. As with Kirk's trial, the Senate hearing did not result in any punitive action against those who took the ballots and lynched the prisoners at Brenham in what became remembered by some as a "pogrom-like attack on African-American families at Old Washington."[139]

Moore proved right in anticipating the demise of the Republicans in Washington County, but not in Washington. The Democrats swept the county in the 1890 elections, but a majority of the ballots cast at Washington were against James S. Hogg for governor and Roger Q. Mills for Congress. Kirk hosted a barbecue in November 1890 at Chappell Hill to thank the black voters there for voting Democratic, but no such celebration was held at Washington. After all, it really no longer mattered how Washington voted. Moore lost his bid for another term as a legislator, but this may have been the least of his concerns. In 1878, when he won his race for the county commission, he was one of two black commissioners, and there were two black constables. In 1890 there was just one black commissioner, George W. Brown, and he drowned in New Year Creek in January 1890 just a few weeks after Moore's house burned to the ground. Moore was appointed to serve in Brown's place until after the fall elections, and then remained in local, not state, politics for the remainder of his public career. He served as a justice of the peace at Washington in the late 1890s, focusing on rent reforms and fencing laws, and from 1901 to 1906 he was the postmaster for Washington.[140]

All of this political turmoil undermined efforts at economic recovery in Washington after the Civil War. Some did not even try. Although they apparently retained a great fondness for the community, many prominent citizens left Washington in the years immediately after the war. Several newspapers, especially those in Houston, announced the demise of the community after so many departed. John D. Rogers, the former commander of the Dixie Blues, always kept a home in Washington, but he moved to Houston. George W. Crawford relocated to Galveston and resumed his shipping trade. After he died there in 1869, his body was buried in a Masonic ceremony at Washington. His erstwhile competitor in politics and journalism, Joseph Lancaster, settled in Navasota, and then moved to Austin. With so many community leaders gone, the last Masonic organization at Washington, Brazos Lodge No. 8, officially closed in 1887, but it had actually submitted its final report ten years earlier.[141]

A Houston correspondent wrote in June 1871 that "places relying upon foreign trade, or so-called natural advantages, will find themselves cut off, run around and left to perish in their ruins, even as the town of Washington on the Brazos has perished." Those who actually stayed in Washington had a different perspective. W. S. Adair arrived in 1875 and found four hundred to five hundred people living there. The *Brenham Weekly Banner* in 1877 reported three hundred residents with lawyers, doctors, and merchants present. The Baptist, Presbyterian, and Methodist churches were open, and the ferry still operated. In April 1871, Edward T. Randle and C. D. Harn had incorporated as the Navasota Ferry Company. The next month they amended their charter, expanding the venture's name to Navasota and Washington County Ferry Company and adding a co-investor: Matthew Gaines, a prominent black Republican legislator. Three years later, an iron bridge was completed across the Brazos, thanks to Harn. As a Republican delegate from Navasota, he introduced a resolution into the 1868 Texas Constitutional Convention for incorporating the Navasota, Washington, and Brazos Bridge Company. He intended to build a toll bridge to link Washington by road to the rail line at Navasota. His effort did not succeed immediately, but in 1870, when he was a state representative, he secured passage of a bill for the same purpose. He died in 1876 before the project was completed, but by 1880 the toll bridge was in place at a cost of $30,000, two-thirds of which was paid by Washington merchant James P. Baldridge. Adair recalled that the bridge diverted some wagon traffic from Brenham to Navasota, but it was not very profitable. Perhaps this was because Fayette Smith, who had come to Washington with his mother in 1841 after Comanches killed his father and sold him to New Mexico traders on his ninth birthday, persisted in operating the ferry after failing to have a narrow gauge railroad built from Washington to Navasota.[142]

Dreams of improving the Brazos and bringing back the steamboats persisted for another fifty years. Congress paid for a survey in 1874 with an eye to improving navigation from Waco to the coast. The engineer in charge, having endured many hardships, strongly urged the federal government not to bother. Yet Congress paid for another survey of the Brazos in 1895, and from this emerged the idea of a system of locks and dams. The estimated cost was $3 million, with the first set of locks to be built just above Washington, at Hidalgo Falls. Efforts may have been underway by 1899, when a summer flood wiped out many farms along the river. Nonetheless, a writer for the *Dallas Morning News* in October of that same year reported that new plans were being laid for clearing obstructions and improving navigation from Velasco on the Gulf Coast to Washington. The cost of locks and dams on this section of the river alone, which was 257 miles in length, were now estimated to be as much as $4 million, but the writer opined that this would be a "mere bagatelle" compared to the economic benefits. Work continued until 1913, when an even worse flood, which "destroyed all standing crops and much of the wealth from Waco to the Gulf," almost put an end to the project. The same flood destroyed the bridge from Washington to Navasota, which had to be repaired at a substantial cost. After ten more years of hard work to keep the channel clear from Washington to Velasco, federal officials stopped the dredging, noting the absence of commercial traffic on the river.[143]

While efforts to revive Washington's economy faltered, the population continued to decline. Although the community was not "silent and almost deserted" in 1881, as a Galveston correspondent wrote, it had shrunk to a small fraction of its former size. The 1880 census found one hundred people living in Washington, of whom fifty-one were white and forty-nine were black. Most of the whites were Anglos born in the United States, and they dominated the non-farming occupations. Alfred D. Gee was the resident constable, Samuel H. Smith was a doctor, Pope Melton had a dry goods store, Thomas W. Neal was a retired physician whose son John H. Neal also practiced medicine, James Devan was a retired merchant, and Joseph J. Wyatt was the justice of the peace. Among the blacks, erstwhile politician Robert J. Moore worked as a pub-

Snag boat *Navasota* on the Brazos River, 1911. *Courtesy Dallas Historical Society. Used by permission.*

lic school teacher and Stephen Davis was a blacksmith. But this makeup soon began to change. Thomas W. Neal's son George D. Neal, who attended Baylor University, married at Washington in 1880 but relocated to Navasota before being elected to the legislature and serving as lieutenant governor. Wyatt, the justice, sold his cotton gin in 1880. Perhaps most interesting, William F. Buckley Sr. was born in Washington in 1881, and the next year his parents moved west to Duval County, whence he attended the University of Texas and later made a fortune in oil. When *Life* magazine on December 18, 1970, published a story that described Buckley's birthplace as being on the Rio Grande, only a few Texans protested that they knew different.[144]

Texas business directories, produced to provide a positive image of the state and lure new residents and investors, blithely reported Washington's population at about twice its actual level in 1884 and 1890, but they also provided other interesting information for astute readers. There were two steam-powered mills for grinding grain and ginning cotton in 1884, then one in 1890. Four general stores and a grocer in 1884 became one general store six years later. The saloon keeper, J. S. Dill, appeared in both publications, but ferryman Smith of course disappeared by 1890. Oddly, one blacksmith became two (one of whom was the enterprising C. P. Monroe, who had bought many of the empty town lots), and two doctors became four, while the town wagon maker persisted. There was no dentist; the last one recorded as living in town drowned himself in the Brazos after only a few months in the community. And Constable Gee shot and killed Dr. George Moeller, a "traveling dentist," in January 1882. Gee escaped but was arrested in Bell County; he need not have bothered: a trial jury acquitted him after reports surfaced that Moeller had threatened to kill Gee after an earlier scuffle. Gee apparently stayed in Bell County, where he died in a gunfight with a deputy marshal at Temple in May 1884. Washington residents had to follow this saga in newspapers published outside their community; no one published a paper in Washington after Lancaster left during the Civil War.[145]

Texas business directories in the late nineteenth century also noted that Washington had at least two schools. Education after the Civil War in Texas received more government support, but school administration remained a local matter, resulting in wide variations in facilities and staffing. State legislation in 1870 led the Washington County commissioners court to divide each of the county's five justice precincts into two school districts, one for whites and one for blacks, with three trustees for each precinct. The first precinct, which included Washington, had three teachers under this system: Methodist minister Caleb L. Spencer, B. F. Wilson (who taught at the Masonic Academy before the Civil War), and Nelson T. Davis. To pay for schools, a property tax was levied in 1874. The next year, incorporated towns were allowed to establish independent school districts. Brenham became the first in the state. Within a year, a related law provided for the creation of "school communities," which resulted in the organization of 92 such entities by 1882 in Washington County and 102 by 1901. Local trustees directed these schools; there was no county superintendent until 1907, and he did not gain direct control by the creation of school districts until 1911. Although thousands of school-age children lived in Washington County during this period, the usual situation became one teacher in each school, white or black. At Washington, Jennie C. Randle, widow of Edward T. Randle, had the only school in 1878. In 1901 the schools for white children in the first precinct were Brown's Prairie, Union Grove, and Felder. Those for blacks included Washington, Paul Felder, Mount Zion, Goodwill, and Brown College.[146]

As many as three churches were supposed to be operating in Washington during the 1880s, according to the directories. This certainly did not include St. Paul's Episcopal Church. The Reverend Robert S. Seeley began holding his primary services at Navasota in 1866, and then had the sanctuary physically moved from Washington to Navasota in 1870. Bishop Alexander Gregg sold the Episcopal parsonage at Washington in 1871. Nor did it include Ruter Chapel, built by the Methodists during the early 1850s. What was left of it was dismantled in 1872 under the supervision of the Reverend Caleb L. Spencer, who sold the old bricks for $500. He donated the bell, which had been given in memory of Martin Ruter by women in Pittsburgh, to a new church in Navasota. He spent part of his proceeds in 1881 on an iron fence to protect Ruter's grave, while other portions helped pay for new parsonages in Independence and Navasota. Spencer himself relocated in 1887 to Navasota, where in 1899 he had Ruter's body reburied in Oakland Cemetery. After he failed to convince Methodist Episcopal Church South officials to pay for a monument to Ruter, Methodist Bishop Willard F. Mallalieu of Massachusetts provided the funds. Mallalieu explained: "This enterprise is a bit of practical fraternity. We cannot have too much of it."[147]

There may have actually been three churches operating in Washington about 1890, but only one dated to the antebellum era. The Presbyterian "small frame church," built in 1849, still operated in 1891, when caretaker William R. Lott wrote that it was used "by all denominations when we have services at all." J. W. Miller, who served as pastor from 1849 to 1873, had never been replaced, and by 1891 Lott and his wife were the last members of the congregation. He added sadly in a memoir penned that year: "Nothing else left but this old Church, and the fond recollections associated that cluster around the sacred spot." His brother Jesse B. Lott, who had been the postmaster at Lott's Store during the election violence of 1886, had become a sponsor for black churches in Washington.

Washington before the fire of 1912. *Courtesy of Star of the Republic Museum, Blinn College, Washington-on-the-Brazos State Historic Site, Washington, Texas.*

He donated land in March 1867 to the trustees of both the African Methodist Episcopal Church and the Colored Baptist Church, and in 1910 he gave five acres to Mount Pleasant Baptist Church. Both brothers, who were the sons of former mayor Robert A. Lott and served together in the Dixie Blues, moved to Navasota around 1890, further reducing support for churches in Washington. Many began attending Friedens Lutheran Church, which was established in 1884 just outside of town in an old Baptist church building.[148]

While Washington continued to serve as a business and social center for the region's farms, visitors saw little that indicated a substantial town. R. A. F. Penrose Jr. in 1880 found houses boarded up and grass growing in the streets. He saw four old men sitting at a table in the middle of a former street drinking whiskey and playing checkers. One had a store in a nearby "shanty." A newspaper reporter in 1899 was kinder, describing Washington as a "small hamlet, with a post-office and one or two small business houses. What was once Main street, is now an ordinary looking wagon road, flanked here and there with an old frame house, and the

remains of brick business structures that once adorned the street."
That same year, however, John S. Barton declared in a *Dallas Morning News* article that Washington lay in ruins "like some sinaccursed Babylon." By 1914 writers used words such as "deserted," "desolate, and "forgotten" to describe Washington. Local historian May A. W. Pennington, who wrote under her married name of Mrs. R. E. Pennington, expanded upon this theme in her county history published in 1915. She wrote: "Today there is nothing left but a few old buildings fast tottering to the end, and one store, which supplies the wants of the adjacent farmers." She added that "brick foundations, old cisterns, and the debris of what was once a commercial center" made it hard to cultivate farms at Washington. Such decline reflected that in nearby communities. John Alexander Sr., a native of Scotland, served as postmaster at Washington from 1866 until his death in 1897. He reported in 1895 that he handled the mail for six other towns that had their post offices closed. This consolidation continued after he died: the Frieden post office closed in 1897, while those at Graball and Lott (formerly Lott's Store) did the same in 1908. All had their mail assigned to Washington.[149]

Little changed in Washington after the turn of the century, except for one important feature. The census taker for the first precinct of Washington County in 1910 might have agreed with Penrose, Barton, and Pennington. But while his rolls did not contain any clear delineation of Washington, they do reveal an interesting shift. He divided the precinct into two parts. One had 1,574 people, all black, and almost all farmers or farm laborers. The other portion contained 379 people, of whom 315 were German (both of their parents or grandparents were German or German Americans born in Texas), 43 were Anglos, and 11 were black. The remaining people living in this part of the precinct were seven Hungarian Romanians and three German Poles. Within this smaller part of the population were diverse occupations that indicated a surviving community: two German Texan schoolteachers (Otto Muery and Henry Bohne), three merchants (Gustav Stolz, Albert Krueger, and George Whitson), a blacksmith (Gustave Aurhr), a Lutheran minister (Fritz Lueckhoff at Friedens Church), a road gang supervisor (Sam S. Bolton), a store clerk (H. P. Henderson), postmaster Louis Kohlfarber, and county commissioner William H. Buck. Even more interesting is that Washington, like much of the surrounding area, had shifted from Anglo to German dominance. Banker D. C. Giddings Sr. of Brenham in 1906 claimed that four out of five residents of Washington County were "Germans and Bohemians," whom he praised as hardworking and thrifty. Nannie Hope of Washington had written to a friend in 1883 that it would be easy for her father to sell his farm because there were lots of Germans in the area looking to buy land. She was right. The founding in 1898 of the Washington Lodge of the Sons of Hermann, a fraternity for men of German descent, underscored this point.[150]

What remained of Washington almost disappeared in 1912, but again the town survived. A terrific fire erupted in November, destroying all but two stores. It began before daylight in Stolz's store and saloon and spread rapidly, consuming Stolz's operation as well as another saloon, a rival store, at least two restaurants, a blacksmith shop, and the old Masonic Hall. Rumors flew that Independence Hall had also burned, but it had already been lost decades earlier. All that was left of Washington's business district after the blaze was two small stores and the post office. Since apparently no one had insurance, the prospects for rebuilding appeared grim. But within months the Bryan newspaper reported that new "fireproof buildings" had been constructed for Stolz's store and several other businesses. By June 1914, when the local chapter of the Woodmen of the World joined with the Sons of Hermann to host a public barbecue at Washington, the community had a cotton gin again, and its population of about one hundred people included a doctor. Local citizens could watch movies in the Sons of Hermann Hall in town, while Friedens Church provided religious services, including frequent weddings.[151]

Being German led to controversy at Washington in World War I. Friedens Church, like many organizations in Washington County and elsewhere, was active in contributing to the Red Cross for Germany early in the war, but attitudes later changed, especially after the United States entered the conflict. In the late summer of 1918, postmaster Louis Kohlfarber was arrested for tampering with mail addressed to the Office of the Provost Marshal General of the United States Army, a criminal investigation agency primarily charged with overseeing the draft at that time. Kohlfarber was sixty-three years of age, born in Germany, and, thanks to mandatory service laws in his native country, a veteran of the German army. He had moved to

Washington after the fire of 1912. *Courtesy of Star of the Republic Museum, Blinn College, Washington-on-the-Brazos State Historic Site, Washington, Texas.*

the United States in 1883 at the age of twenty-eight and became a naturalized citizen at the age of forty. While living in Washington, he blew off two of his fingers with a firecracker at Christmas in 1906, which restricted his work choices, so he became a postmaster. Removed from office, arrested, indicted, and convicted, he was sentenced to three months in jail by the federal district court in Austin. He always claimed that he did nothing but try to repair some envelopes that arrived at his post office already opened. His neighbors may have believed him; according to the 1920 census, he had settled once more in Washington, although he was unemployed.[152]

The 1920 census also revealed other interesting information about Washington. Otto Schroeder, a twenty-seven-year-old schoolteacher who served as the enumerator for his home county of Washington, reported that Washington still had 100 people, 69 of whom were white and 31 were black. Of the former, 59 were German or of German ancestry. One exception was postmaster John R. Alexander Jr., who was Scottish and the son and namesake of the fellow who served as postmaster at Washington from 1866 to 1897. Few among the 100 listed an occupation other than farmer or farm laborer. Among those who did were Nic Sturm, painter; Gus F. Stegemuller, merchant; and T. B. "Ben" Conner, a sixty-one-year-old Texan of German descent who served as the "superintendent," or keeper, of the new state park. There were also three blacks who worked as blacksmiths: Jacob Zepher, P. R. Allen Jr., and Allen's daughter, Merline Doran. Schroeder listed an additional 200 people who used the "Washington Voting Box," of whom 31 were white and 169 were black. Of the 31 white residents, 28 had German parents or grandparents, while A. T. Kramer was listed as a Missouri native who was married to a German Texan. There were also a few other Germans in the surrounding countryside, including former postmaster Kohlfarber, his wife Minnie, and their ten-year-old son. Almost all of those with an occupation in the area around Washington, white or black, were farmers or farm laborers. In sum, Germans and their descendants remained a majority in Washington, but the proportion of blacks was increasing, and more people made their living in agriculture.[153]

Schools can be a strong anchor for a community, and in 1921 Washington got the first rural high school ever constructed in the county. Ten years earlier, when the number of school communities in Washington County had grown to 107, the Texas legislature had moved toward greater efficiency by abolishing them and creating school districts under county boards. The same legislation provided for rural high schools to serve areas that lay outside of incorporated towns. Under this system, by 1918 there were six schools for blacks operating in the district that included Washington. Brown College, which had been in a school community at Washington, occupied a new building in a separate district. There were two schools for whites: Old Union and Brown's Prairie. The latter began with classes taught in Friedens Church by the minister, then a teacher was hired in 1904, and a separate building was constructed in 1912. By 1914 Brown's Prairie School had become a noted educational center. On San Jacinto Day that year, it hosted one of the three institutes for black teachers held in Washington County. Allegedly about one thousand attended. For several years Brown's Prairie and Old Union held a joint annual picnic, and teachers, such as census-taker Schroeder, often taught at both schools. The decision to make Brown's Prairie a rural high school meant the construction of a new three-room building to hold both the primary and secondary grades, and Old Union pupils merged into the student body of Brown's Prairie. Elsie Grebe, a Blinn College graduate who taught at Brown's Prairie before the merger, served as principal of the new school; Hilda Eben, who also graduated from Blinn and previously taught at Brown's Prairie, supervised the secondary classes; and Artie Maxwell taught the elementary pupils.[154]

Brown's Prairie School became commonly known as Old Washington School, but it was not the only consolidated educational facility at Washington by the close of the 1920s. A school for black students was constructed in 1927 "on the edge of Old Washington." It had 102 pupils attending classes in two class rooms and "one room for industrial courses." Eva Marsh Wade, a graduate of Navasota High School and Prairie View A&M College (later University) served as the principal, while there was one other teacher: Phyliss Scales Williams, a Washington County native who also graduated from Prairie View. With the renovation of Brown's Prairie School using Works Progress Administration funds, Washington had two schools, white and black, through the 1930s and 1940s. The Gilmer-Aikin Laws in 1949 then mandated a statewide consolidation of rural schools, hundreds of which closed during the following two decades, and the Civil Rights movement brought an end to racially segregated education. Improvements in transportation allowed more Washington children to attend schools in Brenham and Navasota, so Brown's Prairie School (Old Washington) closed. Friedens Church, which ironically had established Brown's Prairie School, bought the building to be used as a communal hall for classes, meetings, and events.[155]

The building of a new black school at Washington in 1927 may have been a practical recognition of yet another shift in the demography of the community. George W. Crawford's daughter, Kathleen Emma Crawford Randle, visited the site of her old home in Washington in 1921 and remarked: "A few German families— one or two Americans and a few negroes are all that remains." Others echoed her sentiments about the disappearance of many of the buildings and streets, but a writer for the Works Progress Administration in the 1930s updated Randle's comments about the racial composition of her hometown, describing Washington as a "down-at-the-heels country village largely populated with Negroes of the old plantation type; the women, clad in formless 'Mother

Hubbards' and wearing sunbonnets, gossip over rickety fences or sit quietly on rickety porches, smoking their pipes." In fact, of the 111 people in the 1940 census for Washington, 79 were black and 32 were white. Most of the blacks were farmers or farm laborers, while the whites, most of whom had German surnames, dominated other occupations. Gus F. Stegemuller still owned and operated a grocery store, just as he had in 1920, while his son and namesake operated a "retail liquor" store. Five other men worked as store clerks: Henry Boenker, Ennis Denton, Isaac Pollard, Henry Randerman, and Walter Randerman. Willie Stolz was the proprietor of a "private business," while Arnold Wegboest was a bookkeeper for a "private store." Herbert Stolz was a salesman, Henry Brockermeyer was a blacksmith, and Robert D. Fielder was a mechanic in a garage. Minnie Kohlfarber, the widow of the former postmaster, served as the town's telephone operator. Blacks who did not work on farms included Jacob Zepher, a blacksmith (a holdover from the 1920 census like Stegemuller); Thomas Flanagan, a cook in a local café; and Scott Franklin, Floyd Venable, and Jack Moore, all of whom were automobile mechanics. Franklin's wife, Alice, and Flanagan's wife, Oweta, were public school teachers.[156]

World War II, which transformed Texas in many ways, had little impact on Washington. Postmaster Edwin C. Dickschat told a reporter in 1947 that he still served a community of three hundred with the help of his brother William H. Dickschat, a veteran who had fought in the Battle of the Bulge. Obviously Edwin was referring not only to the population of Washington proper, but also the surrounding communities that relied on his post office. Apart from the closing of the schools in Washington, the greatest change after the war came when wealthy urban businessmen, along with other professionals and retirees, began buying farms in Texas rural counties as tax shelters and vacation homes. For Washington, the influx came from Houston, much to the unhappiness of locals who wanted their children to continue working the land and referred to the newcomers as the "mink and manure set." But Texas agricultural production was declining, many blacks were moving elsewhere in search of jobs, and even Germans were willing to sell. The downturn in the Texas economy during the early 1980s slowed the influx of gentlemen farmers, but it never stopped. Fortunately for Washington, many of the new arrivals were as interested in the

Washington in the early 1960s. From R. Henderson Shuffler, "The Signing of Texas' Declaration of Independence: Myth and Record," *Southwestern Historical Quarterly* 65 (April 1962).

history of the region as they were in scenery or farming, and so the community actually got a boost from their arrival as some became involved in preserving and commemorating the place where the Republic of Texas was born.[157]

Dallas Morning News columnist Frank X. Tolbert came to Washington in the late 1950s while working on a series of articles about the capitals of Texas. His first reaction was not very positive, and he remarked that the community was "well-supplied" with taverns. But something hooked him, and he returned several times during the 1960s to talk more with locals about life in Washington, although he still could not avoid mentioning in 1966 that he was conducting his interviews in a "combination general store, meat market, café, and beer tavern." R. Henderson Shuffler saw more, writing in 1965 that while the "biggest store in town" was a liquor store, Washington had a grocery that sold barbecue, a hardware store, two garages, and a post office. Ten years later, a reporter for *Texas Monthly* noted that in addition to the small store that still offered groceries, barbecue, beer, and gasoline, there remained a garage and even a restaurant. In other words, Washington continued to serve as a commercial and social center for a much reduced community.[158]

Washington in 2015 has few of the institutions that delineate a community. Other than the state park that sprawls adjacent to it, the only obvious government presence is a tiny post office. There are no schools or churches on the old townsite, but several churches in the area have a Washington address because that is the closest post office. Most notable among these are Friedens Church (formerly Lutheran, now Church of Christ) and Blessed Virgin Mary Catholic Church (which claims to be the oldest African American Catholic church in Texas). Friedens Church, which has more than 325 members, uses the old facility of Brown's Prairie School as a communal hall, and next to it stands the Washington Volunteer Fire Department. The Sons of Hermann Hall has moved to a site outside of Washington, but it continues to host a barbecue twice each year, in April and October, for the community.[159] Only a few commercial buildings remain on the old townsite, among a scattering of mobile homes and modest houses. One of these is a small store that now serves as a restaurant that is only open on weekends and special occasions. The most substantial reminder of the town and its historic past is the state historic site, whose story began as the community struggled during the early twentieth century.

Washington Post Office. *Public domain image uploaded on Oct. 20, 2008, available at https://en.wikipedia.org/wiki/Washington-on-the-Brazos,_Texas (accessed Sept. 30, 2015).*

Chapter 6
STATE HISTORIC SITE

When county historian May A. W. Pennington wrote about Washington in 1915 that "nothing remains but the shadowy memories of a haunted past, and a shaft of gray Texas granite," there was not much evidence to contradict her. The town had declined until it was little more than a crossroads agricultural community, with a few businesses that served local farmers. But it did have its memories and its historical significance. During the twentieth century and into the next, state officials and new immigrants capitalized on that, refusing to let the past be lost. Even more important, for state officials Washington became an important part of efforts to promote the heritage of the Republic of Texas in place of Confederate Texas in public memory, and thus supplant the Lost Cause with a more regionally inclusive and positive legacy.[160] While their motives often focused on economic development, which included trying to lure tourists as farming and other enterprises became less profitable, the result was that Washington survived as a state-sponsored historic site.

The Fourth of July became a regular occasion for celebration in Washington during the 1890s. The first recorded public gathering for the Fourth was on July 6, 1890, a day chosen so it would not conflict with any other events. The Washington German Brass Band hosted a "grand German fest and ball" at a "pavilion" one mile from town that year. They held another "Grand German Feast and Ball," in conjunction with the Brenham Silver Band, in October of that year at another site close to Washington, presumably in honor of Oktoberfest. County Judge Lafayette Kirk was the main speaker at the following year's celebration on July 3, 1891, when the "meats were well barbecued and in great abundance." That year's program also included Maj. Walter N. Norwood, who served in the Dixie Blues during the Civil War and had since moved to Navasota, and James P. Buchanan, an 1889 graduate of the University of Texas law school and justice of the peace for Washington who was a rising star among local Democrats. By 1897, the event had become a picnic on the banks of the Brazos River jointly sponsored by Washington and the nearby town of Whitman.[161]

A special commemoration was planned for the Fourth of July in 1899. Superintendent E. W. Tarrant of the Brenham Independent School District initiated a fund drive to place a marker at the site where Independence Hall was thought to have stood in Washington, or as close to it as possible. His high school students conducted a fund drive, but program plans were directed by the Texas Independence Monument Association, organized on March 18, 1898, in a meeting of "old settlers" at the Exchange Hotel in Brenham. George H. Wilson served as the president; Beauregard Bryan, grand-nephew of Stephen F. Austin and a judge in Brenham, was among the members. The initial idea was to dedicate the Texas granite shaft, which was twenty feet high and made by R. T. Jaeggli and Jacob Martin of Brenham, on March 2, 1899, but it was not ready in time. A second dedication was scheduled for July 4, 1899, but heavy rains and flooding forced another delay. Finally all was perfect for a ceremony on San Jacinto Day, April 21, in 1900. The marker actually had a date of July 4, 1899, on it, but no one seemed to care. Rufus C. Burleson, president emeritus of Baylor University, delivered an invocation, while Alexander W. Terrell, a former Confederate officer and Texas legislator, gave the keynote address. Two recent graduates of Central High School in Brenham performed an unveiling: Mollie White Harrison, Class of 1897, removed a Lone Star flag draped over the monument, while Frank H. Dever, Class of 1896, officially received the marker. A "Texas barbecue and basket dinner" was then served to all attendees. The new monument stood on private property, but the county commissioners paid to have the area graded and an iron fence installed.[162]

Perhaps concerned about reports of vandalism at the monument, May Pennington in early 1914 suggested the idea of a state park at Washington to the Young Men's Business Association (YMBA) of Brenham. This fit with the ideals of Progressivism: using government to solve a problem and at the same time promoting business.

1899 Monument with iron fence. *Courtesy of Star of the Republic Museum, Blinn College, Washington-on-the-Brazos State Historic Site, Washington, Texas.*

The YMBA embraced the park as part of a scheme to establish an electric railway for tourists from Brenham to Washington as well as lines to other points. They sent a resolution asking the legislature to set aside funds for the project in April 1914. Among those who wrote to support the plan was Rebecca J. Fisher, state president of the Daughters of the Republic of Texas and widow of Orceneth Fisher, the last chaplain of the Senate for the Republic of Texas at Washington. When there was no immediate state response, YMBA representatives met with Gov. Oscar B. Colquitt, trying to convince him to use official influence on their behalf.[163]

Tragedy facilitated the transfer of the property that would become a park, which included the land on which the monument stood, from private hands to state control. The owner of most of the property in question, Gustav Stolz, a forty-one-year-old merchant from Germany who had briefly served as postmaster at Washington, was found dead in front of his store on the night of August 15, 1914. He had closed his business about nine thirty and gone across the street to see a movie at the Sons of Hermann Hall with his clerk. Hearing shots from the direction of the store, he and the clerk investigated and found nothing. The clerk then headed to the Stolz home, where he lived, but as he arrived, he heard six shots. Hurrying back to the store, he found Stolz lying dead in the road, an unfired revolver in his right hand. Three buckshot, in his left shoulder, nose, and eye, had killed him. Ugly reports surfaced that Stolz, who allegedly had the only white-owned store in town at that time, had clashed with local blacks. Twenty-four blacks quickly signed a petition denouncing Stolz's murder and had it published in the *Brenham Daily Banner-Press*, but eight black men were arrested within a week.[164]

The Stolz case became a sensation. The trials of the men who were arrested were to be held on October 6, 1914, but some witnesses did not come and the judge granted a continuance. Two of the blacks indicted in the case were shot and killed that same day while they were eating lunch at the City Café in Brenham; a third black man, not connected to the case, was also shot and died soon afterward. The local coroner decided that there was "very little evidence" for an arrest in the incident, so nothing more was done. The prosecution in the Stolz case began to focus on John Woods, and so his case was moved to Austin for a trial due to concerns for his safety and judicial fairness after the killing of two of his fellow suspects. Two black witnesses came forward and declared Woods was the shooter who killed Stolz, but he was dismissed when his case finally came to trial in April 1915. Three years later, in May 1918, Albert Stolz, whose relation is not known, was shot in the stomach at Washington. No further information appeared in local newspapers. In 1926, Gustav Stolz's twenty-six-year-old son and namesake was shot and killed in his father's store, then operated by his brothers. This time the shooter was Lada Urban, a World War I veteran serving as the postmaster for Washington. Urban told a jury that the shooting was accidental; they agreed and he got a five-year suspended sentence, though he lost his job.[165]

Gustav Stolz was buried at Friedens Church, leaving his widow, Louise Borninghaus Stolz, to support seven children. She made it known that while Gus had not welcomed a sale of his land to the state for a park, she was willing to consider it. The YMBA resumed its campaign in early 1915 with the support of state representative

Sam D. W. Low, a Brenham native whose father had also served in the legislature. Low introduced a bill on March 6 for the appropriation of $10,000 to buy fifty acres for the park and provide for improvements; it passed the Senate but the House adjourned before approving it. Undaunted, Low introduced his proposal again in a special session that convened in late April. Gov. James E. Ferguson sent a note to the legislators on May 5, urging them to approve the bill to purchase and preserve "this hallowed ground, this altar of Texas Independence." Finally the House approved it on May 11, the Senate on May 18, and Ferguson on May 20, 1915.[166]

Ferguson actually visited the park site, for which he had signed the bill to set aside $10,000, twice. The first time was a personal reconnaissance, and presumably a meeting with the widow, during December 1915. He returned on March 2, 1916, the eightieth anniversary of the adoption of the Texas Declaration of Independence, in a much more ostentatious manner. He traveled to Washington from Brenham in a caravan of one hundred automobiles, accompanied by Low, D. C. Giddings, and many other local and state dignitaries. The band of the Second Texas Infantry of the National Guard, along with another band from Navasota, provided music for the crowd of more than two thousand people who attended the ceremony. After Ferguson presented the widow Stolz with a check, President W. B. Bizzell of Texas A&M College (later University), who had been born at Washington, introduced Ferguson for a long speech before barbecue was served to all attendees.[167]

When other claimants surfaced, the state's purchase of the park at Washington became a bit more complicated, which may have slowed its initial development. The widow Stolz and five heirs of ferryman Fayette Smith (Rowland, Roger W., Lena, Edith, and Carrie Smith) sold their land, 32.12 and 17.28 acres respectively, for $60 an acre. Then Adolph A. Chinski contacted state officials and declared that he still owned a town lot on Ferry Street, within the property that had been bought from Stolz's widow. After some discussion, on June 30 Chinski conveyed his title to the state for $100. This left almost $7,000 in the hands of Joseph Owens, commissioner of public buildings and grounds, for improvements. Plans were discussed, but by the end of the first year only two additions had been made: an ornamental iron and steel fence with an arched gateway, fourteen feet high, emblazoned with "Washington Park," and a marble monument commemorating the Ferguson purchase. According to Stella M. Brosig, who later chaired the park board, the site otherwise looked like a "barren waste," so she wrote to Gov. William P. Hobby, who replaced Ferguson after his impeachment, and asked him to appoint a custodian. T. B. "Ben" Conner became the keeper of the park and moved into a "lovely cottage" there in January 1918. He and his wife received an official visit the next fall from two members of the Washington Park Commission, Walker Moore and May Pennington, and several other interested parties: Frederick W. Schuerenberg II, William Lusk (mayor of Brenham), and William A. Yates (Washington County demonstration agent and noted horticulturalist). All of the visitors lived in Brenham except for Moore, who was a resident of Navasota. After a tour, they left with some definite ideas.[168]

The Washington Park Commission in late 1918 declared that $20,000 to $25,000 would be needed for development. Schuerenberg wrote to an earlier successful sponsor, Low, that "we will either make a park out of it or let it remain as it is[,] one of the poorest looking historical spots in the world." But the legislature provided only $1,500 in extra funds for the next year, which Yates and Pennington used to plant pecan trees on the park site. Gov. Pat Neff's veto of the park's operating budget for 1922 may well have sparked some protests, because on March 8, 1923, he signed an act that officially designated the site as "Washington State Park." This bill also created the Washington State Park Commission, with five members to oversee development and operations under the State Board of Control. The measure passed the Senate unanimously, and only one member of the House voted against it. As chair, Neff appointed Brosig, who found that the park looked like it was being used for a farm "with Pigs chickens and Hay field as well as cotton with Bob wire fences." She asked the State Board of Control to visit, which they did. As a result, a professional landscape plan was prepared, which led to the park grounds being cleared and leveled.[169]

Brosig with her colleagues planned to build a replica of Independence Hall to serve as a museum. She was not present when it was built, but she accomplished much more. She left the commission while Miriam A. Ferguson was governor and returned after Dan Moody defeated Ferguson and became governor in 1927. By that time the replica had been designed by architects Charles H. Page and

Louis C. Page of Austin and built by Alex S. Griffin, a contractor and former mayor of Brenham. It was supposed to be dedicated on March 2, 1926, but rain forced a rescheduling to April 21 and then June 3, the birthday of Jefferson Davis. Sen. Joseph W. Bailey delivered the keynote address. Then and later there were arguments over the location and appearance of the new Independence Hall; many thought both were wrong. Adina de Zavala, heroine of the fight to save the Alamo, wrote in 1927 to Henry H. Harrington, chair of the State Board of Control, demanding that a more accurate replica be constructed immediately. Brosig probably worried more about unfulfilled plans to build other park amenities, such as a meeting house, campsites, and sidewalks. The commission did pay Yates to add more pecan trees and other plants, as well as a new gate with a cattle guard flanked by concrete posts, and it welcomed the completion of a paved road into the park and an improved roadway around the site. The paved approach was a major boon. By the 1920s the park had become a popular site for history celebrations, but sometimes these had to be canceled due to the terrible condition of the roads to Washington. Schuerenberg wrote to Low in 1918 that the road from Brenham to the park was "fierce." While a concrete highway was completed across the county in 1921, a paved road to Washington was not laid until the early 1930s, when it provided much needed access for more visitors.[170]

The centennial of Texas independence in 1936 renewed interest in Washington, and thus state spending on the park. Thousands of extra dollars for projects were approved by governors Dan Moody and Ross Sterling in the early 1930s, allowing for the construction of a new brick auditorium, but funds for operations remained meager. Austin architects Bertram E. Giesecke and August W. Harris created an expansion plan to be executed by contractor Travis Broesche. The keeper's house was renovated, while an outdoor amphitheater, storage house, sidewalks, tables, benches, and a barbecue pit were added. A power line was strung from Navasota and water lines were installed. Brosig's "crowning event" was a remodeling of the auditorium to honor the "Immortals" who signed the Texas Declaration of Independence. Reconstructed in a colonial style with cream brick and white trim, with six Corinthian columns and French doors on both the east and west sides, the building cost $21,000. Plans were laid for adding as many as 450 acres to

1926 Replica of Independence Hall. *Courtesy of Star of the Republic Museum, Blinn College, Washington-on-the-Brazos State Historic Site, Washington, Texas.*

the park, but the actual purchase proved to be a small fraction of that. Two town lots had been acquired in 1929, making the park a total of fifty acres, and centennial funds were spent to add another twenty-one acres. Another acquisition was Barrington, the former home of Anson Jones and later James P. Flewellen. Purchased by the Texas Centennial Commission, it was moved to the park at Washington in time for the celebration in 1936, although it was not officially dedicated until the next year, on Texas Independence Day.[171]

The Texas Centennial officially opened at Washington State Park on March 2, 1936, with an all-day celebration. It began with a tremendous parade in Brenham led by Alabama-Coushatta Indians on horseback and in regalia carrying the six flags of Texas. The procession included ten high school bands and an estimated five thousand schoolchildren. Allegedly twice that number sang in a children's choir on the park grounds in Washington, where Gov. James V. Allred of Texas and Gov. Philip F. La Follette of Wisconsin spoke to the crowd. Other speakers included consuls for Mexico, Spain, and France. Although the event was plagued by rain, twenty thousand people braved the elements to attend. Among the organizations present was a new group, the Descendants of the Signers of the Texas Declaration of Independence, who resolved to meet at Washington every year on March 2. The primary sponsors of the event were the Brenham Chamber of Commerce and the Buddy Wright Post of the American Legion in Brenham, who also organized the caravan from Brenham to Washington along the newly paved roadway, but many local businesses such as the store still owned by the Stolz family bought advertisements in the programs.[172]

The Buddy Wright Post continued to host the Washington celebration through the entry of the United States into World War II, when the festivities were suspended. Allred spoke each year during his term as governor, as did William Lee "Pappy" O'Daniel and then Coke Stevenson when they served as governors. High school bands and Texas schoolchildren provided the music. The events were always well attended, with crowds numbering in the thousands, and attracted many heritage groups, some of whom made the Washington gathering their major annual event. In 1940, State Rep. Albert Derden launched his gubernatorial campaign with a rally at the park "to symbolize that he was declaring a new independence against the special interests who were supported by the barons of Wall Street." Most of the time, though, Washington State Park was a place for promoting history rather than politics, as when O'Daniel and Allred spoke together at the Texas Independence Day celebration in 1941, one year before the latter, then a federal judge, ran against the former in an attempt to take his seat in the U.S. Senate. And politicians were not always the principal speakers; in 1940, that honor went to President Homer Price Rainey of the University of Texas at Austin. Of course, to keep things balanced, the Texas A&M Corps of Cadets and Aggie Band escorted Governor O'Daniel to the podium that year. Barbecue was usually served, but not always: chili and tamales were provided in 1941, the year that Governor O'Daniel and his wife entered the amphitheater by walking through an archway of swords held overhead by the Ross Volunteers of Texas A&M College.[173]

O'Daniel's first appearance was especially memorable. Beginning in 1936, each annual celebration was dedicated to a specific signer of the Texas Declaration of Independence, and in 1939 the honoree was that document's author, George C. Childress. A sculpture was unveiled of Childress near the replica of Independence Hall on March 2. Architect Donald S. Nelson, who had worked on Fair Park in Dallas, provided a design to the Texas Centennial Commission. The focus was a large bronze statue of Childress by Raoul Josset, whose other works included figures at Fair Park in Dallas, Goliad, and Monument Hill in La Grange. The Childress figure was cast by E. Gargani & Sons of Brooklyn, New York. It stood on a Texas pink granite base, carved by the Rodriguez Brothers of San Antonio, who produced ten such pieces for the State Board of Control during the Centennial. The names of all of the signers of the Declaration were included on the base. Both houses of the Texas legislature recessed to attend the unveiling by Harriet Hall Dowe, Childress's granddaughter. O'Daniel delivered the dedication address, part of which was broadcast statewide by WFAA radio. Unfortunately for him, the governor spoke too long and suffered a terrible sunburn, so he probably did not much enjoy the singing of "Beautiful Texas," his signature song, by a children's choir. Claude Teer, the chair of the State Board of Control, presented the Childress statue to Mrs. E. P. Anderson, chair of the Washington State Park Board. There were other speakers, including Lieutenant Governor Stevenson and Sam D. W. Low (who died about two months later), and telegrams were read from President Franklin D. Roosevelt, Vice President John N. Garner, and U.S. Sen. Thomas Connally.[174]

World War II interrupted the Texas Independence Day celebrations at Washington State Park. Governor Stevenson did speak at a commemoration of the centennial of Texas statehood in June 1946 at the park, hosted by the Buddy Wright Post of the American Legion. The State Board of Control ceded authority over state historical parks to the State Parks Board a few years later, but nothing changed. Local groups discussed plans, but again nothing happened. Then the Brenham Chamber of Commerce in 1954 appointed a committee to revive annual celebrations of March 2 at Washington. Tom S. Whitehead, publisher of the *Brenham Banner-Press*, emerged as a leader of this effort and pushed hard. As a result, the Texas Independence Day Organization (TIDO) met for the first time at Austin in June 1955. Its president was Donald W. Jeppesen, who had relocated from Houston to Brenham; Dr. H. Bailey Carroll of the Texas State Historical Association and University of Texas at Austin was vice president; and Whitehead served as the executive director. The TIDO Board of Advisors included former governor William P. Hobby, incumbent governor Allen Shivers, U.S. Senators Lyndon B. Johnson and M. Price Daniel Sr., and U.S. Rep. Homer Thornberry. A nonprofit corporation chartered by the state of Texas, TIDO's sole purpose was to expand and promote the park and thus once more make it the focus of Texas Independence Day.[175]

The initial plan from TIDO organizers was to raise $1 million for the construction of a museum and monument like that at San Jacinto, except theirs would be tall enough for a beacon on its peak to be seen for one hundred miles. Revenues from a snack bar and souvenir stores located in its star-shaped base, as well as an elevator for sightseers, would support the park. Thornberry, with the support of Johnson and Daniel, secured congressional authorization for minting Texas Distinguished Service Medals to be given to anyone who donated $500,000 to the park at Washington. To launch a fast-paced campaign to raise $1 million in just seven weeks, as announced by Shivers in an executive proclamation, TIDO sponsored a celebration on March 2, 1956. Texas Attorney General John B. Shepperd delivered the keynote address and Herbert P. Gambrell of Southern Methodist University spoke at the rededication of Barrington, refurbished by TIDO after being used as a storage building and even a stable during World War II. These efforts to accelerate donations did not succeed, although the medals were awarded by the Texas Heritage Foundation to deserving Texans for other accomplishments. Regrouping, TIDO leaders in the fall of 1958 announced that the state had approved a $280,000 plan for building a museum along with roads, sidewalks, parking lots, and picnic facilities, as well as a cemetery for Republic of Texas leaders and more replicas of Republic-era buildings. TIDO president George T. Cates of Killeen declared that most of the money would come from private donors, but the state would be asked to contribute.[176]

Daniel as governor spearheaded the continuing efforts of TIDO to secure funding for park development. He spoke at Texas Independence Day celebrations there in 1959, 1960, and 1961. Just as before World War II, apparently the custom was to dedicate each event to a specific signer of the Texas Declaration of Independence. In 1959, the special guest was Jennie Morrow Decker, Sam Houston's granddaughter. Other interesting aspects of that day's events

Entrance to Washington Park in early 1960s. From R. Henderson Shuffler,
"The Signing of Texas' Declaration of Independence: Myth and Record,"
Southwestern Historical Quarterly 65 (April 1962).

included the dedication of a scaled-back "annex" to the Independence Hall museum and the presentation of a check for $170, the
unpaid rent for the Hall, to Miss Jewel Byars of Houston by TIDO
president Cates. She then endorsed it back to TIDO as a gift from
the heirs of Noah T. Byars. Four years later, after leaving the governor's office, Daniel served as master of ceremonies for Secretary
of the Navy Fred Korth, a Texas native who delivered the March
2, 1963, address at Washington State Park. That year, a special ceremony honored John W. Smith, Alamo courier and congressman
for the Republic of Texas, and Asa Brigham, signer of the Texas
Declaration of Independence and treasurer for the republic. Both
had been re-interred in the Washington town cemetery, near the
park, with official state monuments.[177]

TIDO struggled to raise funds; its biggest gift came from Mary
Moody Northen, who gave $30,000. Change came in 1966 when
George P. Red, a Houston attorney and member of the Sons of the
Republic of Texas whose grandfather, George C. Red, settled in
Washington County before the Civil War, became the president of
TIDO. Red, in recognition of the new name that was bestowed on
the park in 1965, changed the name of his group to Washington-on-
the-Brazos State Park Association and kicked it into high gear. Their

Monument and Independence Hall in early 1960s. From R. Henderson Shuffler, "The Signing of Texas' Declaration of Independence: Myth and Record," *Southwestern Historical Quarterly* 65 (April 1962).

announced fund-raising goal became $1.5 million, with a match of the same amount to come from the state. This would be spent on a new museum and replicas of thirty-two Republic-era buildings at the park. Texas Rep. Gus F. Mutscher, a native of William Penn and graduate of Blinn College, followed the advice of Daniel and secured a pledge of $800,000 from the legislature, contingent upon the association raising $200,000 in donations. Red got the required amount from the Houston Endowment Foundation, established by Jesse H. Jones. His successor, Houston attorney and association board member George A. Butler, who was married to Jones's niece, raised another $100,000 in individual donations. Butler was from Iowa, but he shared Red's dedication to Texas history. In fact, he bought and renovated an antebellum home in Gay Hill, near where Red was refurbishing his grandfather's house.[178]

Butler focused first on replacing the Independence Hall replica, which he and others believed was not only inaccurate but also stood on the wrong site. A groundbreaking ceremony took place at the Texas Independence Day celebration in 1968, at which Texas Sen. William N. Patman (son of U.S. Rep. Wright Patman) spoke. Before the work progressed much further, Curtis D. Tunnell, the first-ever state archaeologist, led a team in digging to locate the foundations of the original Independence Hall. At the same time, R. Henderson Shuffler of the Texana Program at the University of Texas at Austin continued to provide historical research to guide their efforts. When all parties seemed reasonably satisfied, archaeologist-historian Raiford Stripling of San Augustine, who had previously directed the reconstruction of Presidio La Bahía, supervised the building of a more accurate replica of Independence Hall on the correct site. The new building, like the original, had hand-hewn oak siding and a hand-split oak shake roof. The 1926 reconstruction, instead of being razed, was given to Peaceable Kingdom Farm, a residence school for artisans and organic farmers near Washington.[179]

Butler next concentrated on building a new museum at Washington-on-the-Brazos State Park. Later named the Star of the Republic Museum, the two-story facility contained twenty-two thousand square feet of useable space, far more than the original replica of

Monument and Independence Hall. Photo by Robert Plocheck. *Courtesy Texas Almanac.*

Independence Hall. Its ground floor was actually in the shape of a star, while the upper floor was a pentagon. Harvin C. Moore and his son, Barry, were the architects for both the museum and a new auditorium, which used parts of the old facility and was named in honor of Jesse H. Jones. Inside the new museum, many treasures donated by people during the years of the park's operation could now be properly displayed, as well as additional items loaned or given by institutions and individuals. Some of the most impressive objects placed on permanent display included the oldest known Texas flag and a well-known painting by Charles B. and Fanny H. Normann, *The Reading of the Texas Declaration of Independence.* Created for the Texas Centennial in 1936 and displayed in the Hall of State at Fair Park in Dallas and at the Texas Capitol in Austin, the painting was brought to the Star of the Republic Museum from the San Jacinto Monument, although it in fact belonged to a prominent Navasota lawyer, Artie M. Fultz Davis.[180]

While Butler promoted the work on Independence Hall and the Star of the Republic Museum, Faith P. Bybee oversaw a restoration of Barrington. Her husband was Charles L. Bybee, a Houston banker and philanthropist who served as president of the Washington-on-the-Brazos State Park Association from 1970 to 1971, between Butler's two terms. The Bybees were dedicated members of heritage groups, among many organizations, and devoted restorers of historic homes and buildings in Texas; one of her most prominent projects was the renovation of Round Top. She took over the Barrington effort from Edna Ross Hacker, who in 1957 organized the Barrington Society and became its first president. Hacker originally was spurred into action by TIDO's fund-raising push and Texas Independence Day celebration in 1956. She led hasty efforts to borrow furniture and plant gardens, as well as build and furnish a doctor's office, in time for the event. As soon as it was over, borrowed materials were returned and people began raising money for a more substantial renovation of Barrington, which included its removal to a better site, the acquisition of furniture actually owned by the family of Anson Jones, and the reconstruction of period outbuildings.[181]

The new facilities at Washington-on-the-Brazos State Park were dedicated on March 1, 1970, in a fittingly grand ceremony. The Texas State Building Commission ceded control of the new construc-

Star of the Republic Museum. *Public domain image uploaded on Oct. 20, 2008, available at https://en.wikipedia.org/wiki/Washington-on-the-Brazos,_ Texas (accessed Sept. 30, 2015).*

Barrington Living History Farm. Public domain image uploaded on Oct. 20, 2008, available at https://en.wikipedia.org/wiki/Washington-on-the-Brazos,_ Texas (accessed Sept. 30, 2015).

tion to the Texas Parks and Wildlife Department (official successor to the State Parks Board), while the operations of the museum were entrusted to Blinn College. George Butler of the Washington-on-the-Brazos State Park Association presided over the festivities, at which speeches were delivered by Gov. Preston Smith and others in the Jones Auditorium. Mary Moody Northen presented a citation of appreciation to Mutscher, then serving as Speaker of the Texas House. Despite persistent rain, several thousand people were present to applaud as Butler proudly announced that $1.1 million had been spent on improvements at the park, including Independence Hall, the museum and auditorium, and Barrington. Other changes had been made as well, such as relocating the Childress statue to the front of the auditorium and placing it on a new base. Butler also assured the crowd that more improvements were planned, such as the long-discussed idea of rebuilding homes and businesses from the period of the early Republic.[182]

Butler continued as president of the Washington-on-the-Brazos State Park Association well into the 1970s. He presided over a ceremony to honor Mutscher in May 1971 at which Governor Smith, Lt. Gov. Ben Barnes, and Texas Railroad Commissioner Byron M. Tunnell all spoke. In accepting a commendation and gifts totaling $5,000, Mutscher warned the public not to be deceived by "false statesmanship." Ironically, within a year he, Smith, and Barnes would be politically derailed by the Sharpstown scandal. Fortunately this stock fraud scandal had little direct effect on the park, where annual celebrations continued on Texas Independence Day. A newspaper reporter observed in 1973 that "Prior to all the puff and pageantry onstage, the Washington State Park site resembled a friendly country carnival, complete with Blinn Junior College band, Boy Scouts and cold drink stands." University of Texas students in Republic of Texas army uniforms fired their muskets and a cannon into a "fierce clump of mesquite trees" to entertain the small crowd, which numbered about two hundred people. The "puff and pageantry onstage" included speeches by Gov. Dolph Briscoe, Lt. Gov. William P. Hobby Jr., and Speaker of the Texas House M. Price Daniel Jr. As they had for many years, the attendees enjoyed barbecue for lunch.[183]

Not everyone was happy with Butler, especially local residents who opposed the growth of the park and resented the fact that he was an outsider. Opponents rallied around Bubba Stolz, proprietor of the Stolz family store and a grandson of Gustav Stolz, who was murdered in 1914. Stolz hinted darkly that there was a link between his grandfather's death and the state's purchase of his land for a park, and he and other longtime residents of German descent did not respond favorably to offers from state officials interested in buying more of their property. Community involvement by park employees, along with the impact of a steady stream of park visitors who spent money in Washington, eroded this opposition. Sherry Humphreys, curator of collections and exhibits at the museum beginning in 1974, became the president of a new Washington Civic Club that hosted an Oktoberfest in the town in honor of the many Germans who settled on the site. Humphreys and her husband, Jerry, also opened an "Emporium" in Washington, selling jewelry that she made as well as his woodcrafts. The impact was obvious: in 1970, when the museum opened, the park had 71 acres; by 1992, when the museum celebrated the opening of a major expansion, the park included 293 acres, and there were no protests.[184]

The main focus of historical interpretation and preservation at the park at Washington became the museum. The first director was John P. Landers of San Antonio, a noted educator, preservationist, and even poet. His successor, John W. Crain, in five years enlarged the archival holdings, began publishing a newsletter, and assumed control of Barrington from the Barrington Society. D. Ryan Smith was the director for ten years, from 1977 to 1987. He focused on more permanent exhibits, new educational programs that attracted thousands of schoolchildren, and expanded living history demonstrations. It was during his term that the facility officially became the Star of the Republic Museum, in 1979. The longest-serving director, and the one who has overseen the most changes, is Houston McGaugh. A 1991 meeting of representatives from the museum, the Texas Parks and Wildlife Department, and the Washington-on-the-Brazos Park Association produced a renovation plan that resulted in a new visitor's center. Built at a cost of $6 million, it included an education and meeting facility in the renovated auditorium. It was dedicated on March 2, 1998, in a ceremony that included a speech by Lt. Gov. Bob Bullock and the cutting of a "Texas-size birthday cake," similar to the one cut by U.S. Sen. Kay Bailey Hutchison during the 160th anniversary celebration in 1996.

Visitor's Center with Statue of George Childress. Photo by Robert Plocheck. *Courtesy Texas Almanac.*

More important, McGaugh accomplished a complete renovation of the museum by 2002. With staff such as curator Shawn Carlson and education curator Anne McGaugh, the museum continued to win awards into the new millennium while hosting Texas Independence Day celebrations, workshops for teachers, and regional history fairs for the Texas State Historical Association. The new era also brought an interactive website to reach a global audience interested in Texas history.[185]

Today Washington has secured its place in the public mind as the birthplace of Texas. Washington-on-the-Brazos State Historic Site, as it is officially known, is the only facility in the state devoted primarily to the history of the Republic of Texas. With 293 wooded acres adjacent to the Brazos River, the park offers many amenities to visitors interested in learning more about the past. The community has almost vanished, swept away by political and economic changes, with the last vestiges of its boom era destroyed in a fire more than a century ago. But the only threat to the park appears to be the river. Despite stabilization efforts, the Brazos continues to attack its own banks, inundating and even eradicating large swaths of rich bottomlands. One casualty became the original base for the Childress statue. Repurposed as a base for a historical marker after its removal from the figure in 1969, the granite block fell into the Brazos after one of its periodic floods. The park, however, survives, and so does the history of Washington. The buildings are gone, but visitors still drive up the road to the museum and visitor's center, and they walk along the interpretive trails by Independence Hall, and most visit Barrington. The revival of Washington Lodge No. 18 of the Scottish Rite Masons, which meets in Independence Hall every year on Texas Independence Day, indicates an abiding interest in the place where Texas became a nation and then joined the United States less than ten years later. Washington never became the commercial success that its founders envisioned, but it secured a political legacy that has far transcended its physical decline.[186]

Entrance to Washington-on-the-Brazos State Historic Site. Public domain image uploaded on Oct. 20, 2008, available at https://en.wikipedia.org/wiki/Washington-on-the-Brazos,_Texas (accessed Sept. 30, 2015).

Appendix
POETRY

To Arms
Noah T. Byars

Boys, rub your steels and pick your flints,
Methinks I hear some friendly hints
That we from Texas shall be driven—
Our lands to Spanish soldiers given.
To arms—to arms—to arms!

Then Santa Anna soon shall know
Where all his martial law shall go.
It shall not in the Sabine flow,
Nor line the banks of the Colorado.
To arms—to arms—to arms!

Instead of that he shall take his stand
Beyond the banks of the Rio Grande;
His martial law we will put down
We'll live at home and live in town.
Huzza huzza!

SOURCE: DeWitt Clinton Baker, *A Texas Scrap-Book* (New York: A. S. Barnes & Company, 1875), 440.

THE GAINES' MILL RACES
Air—Camptown Races
Inscribed to the Dixie Blues, 5th Regiment, Texas Volunteers

Written by Miss T. W.
Washington, Texas

Our country called for volunteers, do dah, do dah,
"Dixie Blues" replied with cheers, do dah, do dah da.
They joined the loved and gallant band, do dah, do dah,
For protection of their native land, do dah, do dah da.

CHORUS—They have gone to Virginia—they have gone to die
 or win;
To the girls they have left behind: Have no fears for them.

They went away on their own accord, do dah, do dah,
No conscript name is their reward, do dah, do dah da;
They fought like Texans always will, do dah, do dah,
At the battle of Gaines' Mill, do dah, do dah da.

CHORUS—They have gone to Virginia, &c.

McClellan run without delay, do dah, do dah,
As soon as the fight commenced that day, do dah, do dah da;
He run away at light'ning speed, do dah, do dah,
When he saw the "Dixies" in the lead, do dah, do dah da.

CHORUS—They have gone to Virginia, &c.

The grape-shot fell so thick and fast, do dah, do dah,
He sought his gunboats for a mask, do dah, do dah da.
McClellan swore he couldn't succeed, do dah, do dah,
While "Stonewall Jackson" was in lead, do dah, do dah, da.

CHORUS—They have gone to Virginia, &c.

"Mirabile dictu!" was the day, do dah, do dah,

Stonewall sent McClellan away, do dah, do dah da.
Long may "Stonewall" and Hood succeed, do dah, do dah,
To run the Yankees at full speed, do dah, do dah da.

CHORUS—They have gone to Virginia, &c.

Dixie Blues, we'll welcome you, do dah, do dah,
To your homes where hearts are true, do dah, do dah da.
May every one that bears the name, do dah, do dah,
Of a "Dixie Blue," be crowned with fame, do dah, do dah da.

SOURCE: *Houston Tri-Weekly Telegraph*, Sept. 17, 1862.

UNTITLED
May A. W. Pennington

Down where the Brazos sings a low, sweet song,
Of the glory of the vanished years
When Washington was once so great and strong
And faced the future with no fears,
There stands a monument of granite gray
To mark a spot of hallowed earth,
And tell of Texas Independence Day
When a nation had its glorious birth.

It's no cloud-capped, lofty, towering spire,
But just a shaft of modest gray.
Erected there by the children's great desire
To commemorate the liberty day.
It marks the tomb of a nation that is dead;
For the Texas Republic is no more,
And her heroes their silent tents have spread,
With all the hosts long gone before.

Sad desolation reigns around this spot,
Twice the capital of a nation;
Its glorious story ne'er will be forgot;

For it is of brave men of every station.
Straight stands the shaft, while Time unrolls her scroll —
And all alone; for everything has gone;
There's nothing left but Fame's bright honor roll,
And the shaft, to tell a nation was born.

On its way to the Gulf the Brazos River goes,
In spring and summer, winter and fall;
Around its banks so high the weesache grows,
And hoary oaks stand grim and tall,
While the monument keeps watch by night and day,
O'er the lonely place where memories tread;
And e'er the river sings along its way,
A requiem for the town that is dead.

SOURCE: Mrs. R. E. [May Amanda Williams] Pennington, *The History of Brenham and Washington County* (Houston: Standard Printing & Lithographing Co., 1915), 106.

NOTES

Chapter 1: PRELUDE

1. Rena Maverick Green (ed.), *The Swisher Memoirs, by Col. John M. Swisher* (San Antonio: Sigmund Press, 1932), 12; *The Texas Almanac for 1857* (Galveston: Richardson & Co., 1856), 137–138; DeWitt Clinton Baker, *A Texas Scrap-Book* (New York: A. S. Barnes & Co., 1875), 284–285; *Washington American*, Mar. 17, 1857; *Biographical Encyclopedia of Texas* (New York: Southern Publishing Co., 1880), 261–262; "Jones, Randal," *The Handbook of Texas Online*, <http://www.tshaonline.org/handbook/online/articles/fjo63 > [Accessed Feb. 26, 2015]; Jack Jackson, "Perez, Juan Ignacio," *The Handbook of Texas Online*, <http://www.tshaonline.org/handbook/online/articles/fpe32> [Accessed Feb. 26, 2015]; "Biography of Jones, Randall, Capt." <http://www.accessgenealogy.com/texas/biography-of-capt-randall-jones.htm> [Accessed Feb. 26, 2015]. Several sources say that James Walker commanded the Brazos River expedition in 1819; see *Galveston Weekly News*, May 13, 1880; *Houston Post*, Apr. 29, 1900; Homer S. Thrall, *A Pictorial History of Texas* (St. Louis: N. D. Thompson & Co., 1879), 136–138, 575; John Henry Brown, *Indian Wars and Pioneers of Texas* (Austin: L. E. Daniell, 1880), 603–604; John Henry Brown, *History of Texas from 1685 to 1892*, 2 vols. (Austin: L. E. Daniell, 1892–1893), II, 74–75; Jonnie L. Wallis and Laurance L. Hill, *Sixty Years on the Brazos: The Life and Letters of Dr. John Washington Lockhart, 1824–1900* (Los Angeles, Calif.: Dunn Brothers, 1930), 12. But this assertion seems unlikely: James Walker Sr. came to Texas in 1824, and James Walker Jr. in 1835. See John G. Johnson, "Walker, James," *The Handbook of Texas Online*, <http://www.tshaonline.org/handbook/online/articles/fwa19> [Accessed Feb. 26, 2015].

2. George R. Nielsen (ed.), "Lydia Ann McHenry and Revolutionary Texas," *Southwestern Historical Quarterly* 74 (January 1971): 399 (quotation; journal cited hereafter as *SHQ*); Eugene C. Barker (ed.), *The Austin Papers* (Washington, D.C.: Government Printing Office, 1924–1928), I, 838–839, 976–977; Stephen L. Moore, *Savage Frontier, Volume I: Rangers, Riflemen, and Indian Wars in Texas, 1835–1837* (Denton: University of North Texas Press, 2007), 18–19; "Robinson, Andrew," *The Handbook of Texas Online*, <http://www.tshaonline.org/handbook/online/articles/fro35> [Accessed Feb. 26, 2015]; Catherine G. Alford, "Oldham, William," *The Handbook of Texas Online*, <http://www.tshaonline.org/handbook/online/articles/fol16> [Accessed Oct. 11, 2015].

3. *Dallas Morning News*, Mar. 30, 1896, Mar. 3, 1929, Feb. 28, 1970; Sue W. Moss, "Description of the Built Environment, Principal Significance, and Important Events of the Three Eras of Washington Townsite" (Typescript), Dec. 14, 1994 (Star

of the Republic Museum, Washington, Texas), 1; Mrs. R. E. [May Amanda W.] Pennington, *The History of Brenham and Washington County* (Houston: Standard Printing & Lithographing Company, 1915), 100; Louis W. Kemp, *The Signers of the Texas Declaration of Independence* (Houston: Anson Jones Press, 1944), x; "Robinson, Andrew."

4. Washington *Texas Ranger and Lone Star* (Washington, Texas), Sept. 10 and 22, 1853; *Statesman* (Austin), Nov. 26, 1899; *Dallas Morning News*, Mar. 3, 1929; Dana Morris Card File (Star of the Republic Museum); Moss, "Description," 1–2, 9; Kemp, *Signers*, x–xi; "Robinson, Andrew"; "Hall, John W.," *Handbook of Texas Online*, <http://www.tshaonline.org/handbook/online/articles/fha20> [Accessed Feb. 26, 2015].

5. *Telegraph and Texas Register* (Houston), Jan. 2 and 30, Nov. 23, Dec. 17, 1836; *Houston Weekly Telegraph*, Feb. 17, Mar. 10, 1838; *Texas Ranger and Lone Star* (Washington), Sept. 10 and 22, 1853; *Dallas Morning News*, Mar. 3, 1929; Ernest W. Winkler (comp.), "Documents Relating to the Organization of the Municipality of Washington, Texas," *SHQ* 10 (July 1906): 96; Morris Card File; Kemp, *Signers*, xi; Moss, "Description," 2–3, Appendix: 10; "Robinson, Andrew"; "Chriesman, Horatio," *The Handbook of Texas Online*, <http://www.tshaonline.org/handbook/online/articles/fch35> [Accessed Feb. 26, 2015].

6. Winkler, "Documents," 96–99; H. P. N. Gammel (comp.), *The Laws of Texas, 1822–1897* (10 vols.; Austin: Gammel Book Co., 1898–1902), I, 245; Ernest W. Winkler, "The Seat of Government of Texas," *SHQ* 10 (October 1906): 141; Pennington, *Washington County*, 31; Moss, "Description," 3; Kemp, *Signers*, 1; "Miller, James B.," *The Handbook of Texas Online*, <http:// www.tshaonline.org/handbook/online/articles/fmi15> [Accessed Feb. 26, 2015].

7. Wallis and Hill, *Lockhart*, 40, 82; Paul Lack (ed.), *The Diary of William Fairfax Gray: From Virginia to Texas, 1835–1837* (Dallas: William P. Clements Center for Southwest Studies, Southern Methodist University, 1997), 98; Moss, "Description," 3–4, 10, 12.

8. *Telegraph and Texas Register* (Houston), May 16 and 30, 1838; *Lone Star and Southern Watch Tower* (Washington), July 5, 1851; *Texas Ranger and Lone Star* (Washington), Mar. 30, 1854; *Dallas Morning News*, Jan. 8, 1897, Sept. 15, 1950; Lewis R. Bryan, "Navigation of the Brazos River, Past and Present, and What is Being Done for the Future," *Texas Department of Agriculture Year Book* (1910), 263; Pamela A. Puryear and Nath Winfield Jr., *Sandbars and Sternwheelers: Steam Navigation on the Brazos* (College Station: Texas A&M University Press, 1976), 14–15, 42–43; John M. Brockman, "Port Sullivan: Ghost Town" (M.A. thesis, Texas A&M University, 1968), chap. 2, <http://www.rootsweb.ancestry.com/~txrober2/books/PortSullivanII.htm> [Accessed Mar. 2, 2015]; Jean L. Epperson, "Cayuga," *The Handbook of Texas Online*, <http://www.tshaonline.org/handbook/online/articles/qtco1> [Accessed Mar. 2, 2015].

9. *Dallas Morning News*, Feb. 28, 1970; Nielsen, "Lydia Ann McHenry," 400 (1st quotation); Mary Austin Holley, *Texas* (Lexington, Ky., 1836; reprint, Austin: Texas State Historical Association, 1985), 118 (2nd quotation); Moss, "Description," 3–8, 10; Winkler, "Seat of Government," 150; Karen Moore, "Mann, Pamelia Dickinson," *The Handbook of Texas Online*, <http://www.tshaonline.org/handbook/online/articles/fma35> [Accessed Feb. 27, 2015].

10. Alex Dienst, "Contemporary Poetry of the Texas Revolution," *SHQ* 21 (October 1917): 157–158 (1st quotation); Charles A. Gulick et al. (eds.), *The Papers of Mirabeau Buonaparte Lamar*, 6 vols. (Austin: Texas State Library, 1920–1927),

II, 166 (2nd quotation); Nancy B. Parker, "Mirabeau Buonaparte Lamar's Texas Diary Edited," *SHQ* 84 (January 1981): 320–321; Stanley Siegel, *Poet President of Texas* (Austin: Pemberton Press, 1977), 39; A. K. Christian, "Mirabeau Buonaparte Lamar," *SHQ* 24 (January 1921): 158, 170.

11. Green, *Swisher Memoirs*, 14, 16–17; Ralph W. Steen (ed.), "A Letter from San Antonio de Bexar in 1836," *SHQ* 62 (April 1959): 513–518; "Robinson, Andrew."

12. Republic of Texas Claims: Noah T. Byars, Texas State Library and Archives, Austin, <https://www.tsl.texas.gov/apps/arc/repclaims/index.php?formType=name &lastName=Byars&firstName=Noah&searchType=beginLike&dosearch=Search+ Now> [Accessed Feb. 27, 2015]; Malcolm D. McLean (comp.), *Papers Concerning Robertson's Colony in Texas,* 19 vols. (Arlington: University of Texas at Arlington Press, 1974-1993), XIII, 61; Herman Ehrenberg, *With Milam and Fannin: The Adventures of a German Boy in Texas' Revolution,* trans. Charlotte Churchill (Austin: Pemberton Press, 1968), 18 (1st quotation); William P. Zuber, *My Eighty Years in Texas* (Austin: University of Texas Press, 1971), 47 (2nd quotation); Lack, *Gray Diary*, 97 (3rd quotation), 98 (4th and 5th quotations); Moss, "Description," 4–5, 8, 10; Kemp, *Signers,* xxvi–xxvii; Charles F. Schmidt, *History of Washington County* (San Antonio: Naylor Press, 1949), 13; R. Henderson Shuffler, "The Signing of Texas' Declaration of Independence: Myth and Record," *SHQ* 65 (April 1962): 314–315; "Find a Grave: Robert Alexander Lott," <http://www.findagrave.com/cgi-bin/fg.cgi?page=pv&GRid=47288381&PIpi=29555904> [Accessed Feb. 27, 2015]; Bill Groneman, "Harrison, William B.," *The Handbook of Texas Online,* <http:// www.tshaonline.org/handbook/online/articles/fhaex> [Accessed Feb. 27, 2015].

13. Eugene C. Barker (ed.), "Journal of the Permanent Council (October 11–27, 1835)," *Quarterly of the Texas State Historical Association* 7 (April 1904): 265; Winkler, "Seat of Government," 143–146; Schmidt, *Washington County*, 7.

14. Lack, *Gray Diary*, 98 (quotations); Gammel, *Laws of Texas,* I, 563–564, 575–576, 802–813, 980–982; Winkler, "Seat of Government," 148–151; Kemp, *Signers,* viii–ix; McLean, *Robertson's Colony,* XIII, 69, 74–79; Ralph W. Steen, "Smith, Henry," *The Handbook of Texas Online,* <http:// www.tshaonline.org/ handbook/online/articles/fsm23> [Accessed Feb. 27, 2015].

15. *Dallas Morning News,* July 26, 1960; Republic of Texas Claims: Byars; Louis E. Brister, "The Journal of Col. Eduard Harkort, Captain of Engineers, Texas Army, February 8–July 17, 1836," *SHQ* 102 (January 1999): 356 (quotations); Lack, *Gray Diary,* 112; Moss, "Description," 5; Kemp, *Signers,* xxii–xxiii, xxv–xxvii; Shuffler, "Signing," 312–314, 316–317; "Dr. William P. Smith, 1795–1870," <http://www. tamu.edu/faculty/ccbn/dewitt/drsmith.htm> [Accessed Feb. 27, 2015]; Ralph W. Steen, "Convention of 1836," *The Handbook of Texas Online,* <http://www. tsha-online.org/handbook/online/articles/mjc12> [Accessed Feb. 27, 2015].

16. Amelia W. Williams and Eugene C. Barker (eds.), *The Writings of Sam Houston, 1813–1863,* 8 vols. (Austin: University of Texas Press, 1938–43), I, 315–318, 330 (quotation); *Texas Almanac for 1860* (Galveston: W. & D. Richardson, [1860]), 42–43; James L. Haley, *Sam Houston* (Norman: University of Oklahoma Press, 2002), 118, 120.

Chapter 2: POLITICAL SEAT

17. Lack, *Gray Diary,* 119; Moss, "Description," 6–7.

18. Lack, *Gray Diary,* 116; Green, *Swisher Memoirs,* 16–17; Haley, *Houston,* 122–123; *Texas Almanac for 1860,* 51; Shuffler, "Signing," 312; Joe E. Ericson, "Ellis, Richard," *The Handbook of Texas Online,* <http://www.tshaonline.org/

handbook/online/articles/fel16> [Accessed Feb. 27, 2015]; Joe E. Ericson, "Childress, George Campbell," *The Handbook of Texas Online*, <http://www.tshaonline. org/handbook/online/articles/fch28> [Accessed Feb. 27, 2015].

19. Lack, *Gray Diary*, 122–123; McLean, *Robertson's Colony*, XIII, 120; Winkler, "Seat of Government," 152–153; *Texas Almanac for 1860*, 51; Jean L. Epperson, "1834 Census, Anahuac Precinct, Atascosito District," *SHQ* 92 (January 1989): 441; Mary W. Clarke, *David G. Burnet* (Austin: Pemberton Press, 1969), 60–63; Stanley Siegel, *A Political History of the Texas Republic, 1836–1845* (Austin: University of Texas Press, 1956), 33.

20. *Dallas Morning News*, Mar. 3, 1929; *Texas Almanac for 1860*, 51; Lack, *Gray Diary*, 124 (1st quote); S. F. Sparks, "Autobiographical Sketch of the Life of S. F. Sparks" (typescript, March 16, 1895), 4 (2nd quotation), 5 (Dolph Briscoe Center for American History, University of Texas at Austin, cited hereafter as CAH); "Recollections of S. F. Sparks," *SHQ* 12 (July 1908): 62–63; Baker, *Texas Scrap-Book*, 59; Winkler, "Seat of Government," 152–153; Haley, *Houston*, 181; Clarke, *Burnet*, 65, 66; Henderson K. Yoakum, *History of Texas from its First Settlement in 1685 to its Annexation to the United States in 1846*, 2 vols. (New York: Redfield, 1856), II, 75, 111; Lois F. Blount, "A Brief Study of Thomas J. Rusk, Based on Letters to his Brother, David, 1835–1856, II," *SHQ* 34 (April 1931): 274; Shuffler, "Signing," 325.

21. Green, *Swisher Memoirs*, 50; *Texas Almanac for 1860*, 51; Winkler, "Seat of Government," 152–153; Moore, *Savage Frontier, Vol. I*, 112–113, 119; Joseph E. Chance, "Chance, Joseph Bell," *The Handbook of Texas Online*, <http://www. tshaonline.org/handbook/online/articles/fch12> [Accessed Feb. 27, 2015].

22. Gerald S. Pierce, *Texas Under Arms: The Camps, Posts, Forts, & Military Towns of the Republic of Texas 1836–1846* (Austin: Encino Press, 1969), 178; Darren L. Ivey, *The Texas Rangers: A Registry and History* (Jefferson, N.C.: McFarland, 2010), 32; "Pierson, John Goodloe Warren," http://www.earlytexasfamilies.com/family/pierson/JGW_Pierson.htm [Accessed Feb. 26, 2015]); "Pierson (Pearson), J. G. W.," <http://www. tshaonline.org/supsites/military/t/pierjg3t.htm> [Accessed Feb. 26, 2015]; Louis W. Kemp, "Barnett, George Washington," *The Handbook of Texas Online*, <http://www.tshaonline.org/handbook/online/articles/fba71> [Accessed Feb. 26, 2015]; Noel Grisham and Louis W. Kemp, "Coles, John P.," *The Handbook of Texas Online*, <http://www.tshaonline.org/handbook/online/articles/fco21> [Accessed Feb. 26, 2015]; James L. Haley, "Hill, William Warner," *The Handbook of Texas Online*, <http://www.tshaonline.org/handbook/online/articles/fhi29> [Accessed Feb. 26, 2015].

23. *Houston Weekly Telegraph*, June 13, 1837; J. H. Kuykendall, "Reminiscences of Early Texans," *Quarterly of the Texas State Historical Association* 6 (January 1903): 246–247; Lucy A. Erath, "Memoirs of Major George Bernard Erath," *SHQ* 26 (January 1923): 275–280; Ivey, *Texas Rangers*, 35; Moore, *Savage Frontier, Vol. I*, 18–19, 227–228; James T. DeShields, *Border Wars of Texas* (Tioga, Tex.: Herald Co., 1912), 216–217; Thomas W. Cutrer, "Robison, Joel Walter," *The Handbook of Texas Online*, <http://www.tshaonline.org/handbook/online/articles/fro42> [Accessed Feb. 26, 2015].

24. *Telegraph and Texas Register* (Houston), Mar. 21, 1837 (quotation), Jan. 27, Feb. 17 and 24, Mar. 10, 1838; *Texas National Register* (Washington), July 3, 1845; *Dallas Morning News*, Mar. 3, 1929; Lack, *Gray Diary*, 216; Wallis and Hill, *Lockhart*, 40, 41, 48; Moss, "Description," 11–12, Appendix: 3–5; "Find a Grave: Thomas Paine Shapard," <http://www.findagrave.com/cgi-bin/

fg.cgi?page=gr&GRid=63301949> [Accessed Mar. 2, 2015]; "History of the Lake Creek Settlement in Texas," <http://www.texashistorypage.com/Lake_Creek_Settlement.html> [Accessed Mar. 2, 2015].

25. Wallis and Hill, *Lockhart*, 40, 41, 48; Morris Card Files; U.S. Bureau of the Census, Eighth Census, 1860, Schedule 1: Free Population (Washington County, Texas), E. S. Cabler, RG 29 (National Archives, Washington, D.C.); Harriet Smither, "Diary of Adolphus Sterne," *SHQ* 33 (July 1929): 77 (quotation); Moss, "Description," 12–13, 15–16, Appendix: 7, 13; "History of the Lake Creek Settlement"; Betty Dunn, "Farquhar Cemetery, Washington County," <http://www.texascenterforregionalstudies.com/farquhar-cemetery-washington-county.html> [Accessed Oct. 26, 2014]; "Caswell County Family Tree," <http://wc.rootsweb.ancestry.com/cgi-bin/igm.cgi?op=GET&db=caswellcounty&id=I3498> [Accessed Mar. 8, 2015]; Schmidt, *Washington County*, 14; "Find a Grave: LTC James Russell Cook, Sr."; "Find a Grave: Thomas Gay," <http://www.findagrave.com/cgibin/fg.cgi?page=gr& GSln=Gay&GSfn=Thomas+&GSbyrel=all&GSdyrel=all&GSst=46&GScntry=4& GSob=n&GRid=17306464&df=all&> [Accessed Mar. 2, 2015]; Thomas W. Cutrer, "Cooke, James Russell," *The Handbook of Texas Online*, <http://www. tshaonline.org/handbook/online/articles/ fco48> [Accessed Feb. 27, 2015]; Carole E. Christian, "Washington-on-the-Brazos, TX," *The Handbook of Texas Online*, <http://www.tshaonline.org/handbook/online/articles/hvw10> [Accessed Feb. 26, 2015]; Norman W. Spellmann, "Ayres, David," *The Handbook of Texas Online*, <http://www.tshaonline.org/handbook/online/articles/ fay05> [Accessed Mar. 2, 2015]; Thomas W. Cutrer, "Travis, Charles Edward," *The Handbook of Texas Online*, <http://www.tshaonline.org/handbook/online/articles/ftr04> [Accessed Mar. 2, 2015].

26. *Dallas Morning News*, May 11, 1902; Yoakum, *History of Texas*, II, 537, 539; Homer S. Thrall, *History of Methodism in Texas* (Houston: E. H. Cushing, 1872), 23; Walter N. Vernon et al., *The Methodist Excitement in Texas: A History* (Dallas: United Methodist Historical Society, 1984), 40, 42, 45, 48; C. C. Cody, "Rev. Martin Ruter, A.M., D.D.," *Texas Methodist Historical Quarterly* 1 (July 1909): 15; Robert Wooster, "Stephenson, Henry," *The Handbook of Texas Online*, <http://www.tshaonline.org/handbook/online/articles/fst40> [Accessed Mar. 7, 2015]; Norman W. Spellmann, "Methodist Church," *The Handbook of Texas Online*, <http://www.tshaonline.org/handbook/online/articles/imm01> [Accessed Mar. 7, 2015].

27. *Dallas Morning News*, May 11, 1902; Yoakum, *History of Texas*, II, 540; Thrall, *Methodism in Texas*, 24; Vernon et al., *Methodist Excitement*, 43; Cody, "Ruter," 10–20; Spellmann, "Ayres, David"; Norman W. Spellmann, "Kenney, John Wesley," *The Handbook of Texas Online*, <http://www.tshaonline.org/handbook/online/articles/fke27> [Accessed Mar. 7, 2015]; Norman W. Spellmann, "Ruter, Martin," *The Handbook of Texas Online*, <http://www.tshaonline.org/handbook/online/articles/fru25)> [Accessed Mar. 7, 2015].

28. *Telegraph and Texas Register* (Houston), May 26, 1838; *Dallas Morning News*, May 11, 1902; Morris Card Files; William P. Smith to B. P. Peel, June 10, 1852, Martin Ruter Papers (CAH); "Record Book of the Trustees for the Church Property of the M.E. Church South at Washington" (manuscript), 1848–1889, n.p. (Star of the Republic Museum); Williams and Barker, *Writings of Sam Houston*, I, 324–325; Vernon et al., *Methodist Excitement*, 45, 48; Macum Phelan, *A History of Early Methodism in Texas, 1817–1866* (Dallas: Cokesbury Press, 1924), 40–41, 92–93, 99, 101; Moss, "Description," Appendix: 8; Cody, "Ruter," 25, 26–32; "Dr. William P. Smith, 1795–1870," <http://www.tamu.edu/faculty/ccbn/dewitt/drsmith.htm> [Accessed Mar 7, 2015]; "Find a Grave: Dr. William P. Smith," <http://www.

findagrave.com/cgi-bin/fg.cgi? page=gr&GRid=30748820> [Accessed Mar. 7, 2015].

29. Wallis and Hill, *Lockhart*, 54; Cody "Ruter," 27; David Ayers, "Reminiscences of David Ayers," *Texas Methodist Historical Quarterly* 1 (July 1909): 43; Randolph B. Campbell, *An Empire for Slavery: The Peculiar Institution in Texas, 1821–1865* (Baton Rouge: Louisiana State University Press, 1989), 173; Robert Edgar Ledbetter Jr., "Fisher, Orceneth," *The Handbook of Texas Online*, <http://www.tshaonline.org/handbook/online/articles/ffi21> [Accessed Mar. 7, 2015].

30. *Telegraph and Texas Register* (Houston), May 30, 1838; Morris Card Files; Zenos N. Morell, *Flowers and Fruits from the Wilderness* (Boston: Gould and Lincoln, 1872), 72, 76 (1st quotation), 77–78; James L. Walker and J. P. Lumpkin, *History of the Waco Baptist Association of Texas* (Waco, Tex.: Byrne-Hill Print House, 1897), 255, 326 (2nd quotation), 369; L. R. Elliott (ed.), *Centennial Story of Texas Baptists* (Chicago: Hammond Press, 1936), 25; Cody, "Ruter," 19; Moss, "Description," Appendix: 2; Steve Sadler, "Morrell, Z. N.," *The Handbook of Texas Online*, <http://www.tshaonline.org/handbook/online/articles/fmo53> [Accessed Mar. 7, 2015].

31. *Dallas Morning News*, Feb. 21, 1900; Morrell, *Flowers and Fruits*, 82–85; Yoakum, *History of Texas*, II, 539; George R. Nielsen, "Mathew Caldwell," *SHQ* 64 (April 1961): 483; Sadler, "Morrell, Z. N."; Louis W. Kemp, "Caldwell, Mathew," *The Handbook of Texas Online*, <http://www.tshaonline.org/handbook/online/articles/fca12> [Accessed Mar. 3, 2015].

32. Wallis and Hill, *Lockhart*, 67; Morrell, *Flowers and Fruits*, 135, 148–149; Walker and Lumpkin, *Waco Baptist Association,* 9; Pennington, *Washington County*, 103; Cody, "Ruter," 19; Elliott, *Texas Baptists*, 30–31; Robert A. Baker, *The Blossoming Desert: A Concise History of Texas Baptists* (Waco, Tex.: Word Books, 1970), 38, 61–63; Harry L. McBeth, *Texas Baptists: A Sesquicentennial History* (Dallas: Baptistway Press, 1998), 32–33; Travis L. Summerlin, "Tryon, William Milton," *The Handbook of Texas Online*, <http://www.tshaonline.org/ handbook/online/articles/ftr19> [Accessed Mar. 7, 2015].

33. *Telegraph and Texas Register* (Houston), Jan. 27, May 26, July 29, 1837; *Dallas Morning News*, Mar. 3, 1929; Wallis and Hill, *Lockhart*, 13, 33–34; Gammel, *Laws of Texas,* I, 296–297; Pennington, *Washington County,* 102; Cecil E. Evans, *The Story of Texas Schools* (Austin: Steck Co., 1955), 56; Frank Brown, "Annals of Travis County and the City of Austin" (manuscript), n.d., chap. 15, p. 22 (CAH); Arthur A. Grusendorf, "The Social and Philosophical Determinants of Education in Washington County, Texas, 1835–1937" (Ph.D. diss., University of Texas at Austin, 1938), 64–65, 80–86, 89–91; "Caswell County Family Tree"; "Thompson, Frances Judith Somes Trask," *The Handbook of Texas Online*, <http://www.tshaonline.org/ handbook/ online/articles/fth19> [Accessed Mar. 8, 2015].

34. *Proceedings of the Grand Lodge of Texas* (Galveston: Richardson & Co., 1857), 27, 43, 54, 116–117, 119, 126, 134, 179–181; Joseph W. Hale, "Masonry in the Early Days of Texas," *SHQ* 49 (January 1946): 376; William Preston Vaughn, "Freemasonry," *The Handbook of Texas Online*, <http://www.tshaonline.org/handbook/online/articles/vnf01> [Accessed Mar. 8, 2015].

35. *Texas National Register* (Washington), Dec. 7, 1844; *Dallas Morning News*, June 13, 1899, Mar. 3, 1929 (1st quotation); Wallis and Hill, *Lockhart*, 13, 33–34 (2nd quotation), 35; Pennington, *Washington County*, 102; Grusendorf, "Education in Washington County," 81–91; "My Family: Lindsey Powell Rucker," <http://www.familyorigins.com/users/s/c/o/David-Wayne-Scott-KS/FAMO1-0001/d38.htm> [Accessed Mar. 8, 2015].

36. *National Vindicator* (Washington), Jan. 13, 1844; *Texas National Register* (Washington), Apr. 17, 1845; *Dallas Morning News,* July 23, 1905; Harriet Smither, "Diary of Adolphus Sterne," *SHQ* 35 (July 1931): 77, 81 (quotation); Richard S. Hunt and Jesse S. Randal, *A New Guide to Texas* (New York: Sherman & Smith, 1846), 62; "Find a Grave: Rev. Benjamin Burdick Baxter," <http://www. findagrave. com/cgi-bin/fg.cgi?page=gr&GRid=69461346> [Accessed Mar. 8, 2015]; Richard B. McCaslin, *Fighting Stock: John S. "Rip" Ford of Texas* (Fort Worth: Texas Christian University Press, 2011), 12; Thomas W. Cutrer, "Swisher, John Milton," *The Handbook of Texas Online,* <http://www.tshaonline.org/handbook/online/articles/fsw20> [Accessed Mar. 8, 2015].

37. *Telegraph and Texas Register* (Houston), Feb. 24. 1838; *Daily News* (Galveston), Mar. 12, 1893; Gammel, *Laws of Texas,* I, 298–99, 1459; Morris Card Files; Pennington, *Washington County,* 14, 31, 105; Schmidt, *Washington County,* 7; Moss, "Description," 14, Appendix: 3, 8.

38. *National Vindicator* (Washington), Nov. 25, 1843 (quotation), Feb. 3, 1844; *Brenham Daily Press,* Sept. 1, 1913; Gammel, *Laws of Texas,* II, 552, 959–960; W. O. Dietrich, *The Blazing Story of Washington County* (Brenham, 1950; rev. ed., Wichita Falls: Nortex, 1973), 17–20, 25; Pennington, *Washington County,* 15, 31–32, 105; Schmidt, *Washington County,* 8.

39. Stanley Siegel, *Big Men Walked Here! The Story of Washington on the Brazos* (Austin: Jenkins Publishing Co., 1971), 39–41, 43–48; Winkler, "Seat of Government," 165; Haley, *Houston,* 242–243, 251–252.

40. Stephen L. Moore, *Savage Frontier, Volume IV: Rangers, Riflemen, and Indian Wars in Texas, 1842–1845* (Denton: University of North Texas Press, 2010), 97; Joseph M. Nance, *Attack and Counter-Attack: The Texas-Mexican Frontier, 1842* (Austin: University of Texas Press, 1964), 342, 412–413, 427, 442, 445; Janelle Holmes (comp.), "Family Tree of Jesse L. McCrocklin," <http://www.rootsweb. ancestry.com/~txblanco/jmccrocklin.htm> [Accessed Feb. 27, 2015]; John S. Morslund, "Blanco County Families for 100 Years," <http://www.texiasllc.com/ blanco-100-years/> [Accessed Feb. 27, 2015]; "Find a Grave: LTC James Russell Cook, Sr.," <http://www.findagrave.com/cgi-bin/fg.cgi?page=gr&GRid=48328066> [Accessed Feb. 27, 2015]; "Find a Grave: Maj Samuel A Bogart," <http://www. findagrave.com/cgi-bin/fg.cgi?page=gr&GRid=59001968> [Accessed Feb. 27, 2015]; Cutrer, "Cooke, James Russell"; Robert Maberry Jr., "Robertson, Jerome Bonaparte," *The Handbook of Texas Online,* <http://www.tshaonline.org/handbook/online/articles/fro28> [Accessed Feb. 27, 2015].

41. *Brenham Daily Press,* Sept. 1, 1913; Sterling B. Hendricks, "The Somervell Expedition to the Rio Grande, 1842," *SHQ* 23 (October 1919): 112–140; Llerena B. Friend (ed.), "Sidelights and Supplements on the Perote Prisoners," *SHQ* 69 (October 1965): 228; Moore, *Savage Frontier, Vol. IV,* 97; Nance, *Attack and Counter-Attack,* 472, 530–532, 534–535; Kaye A. Walker, "Brenham, Richard Fox," *The Handbook of Texas Online,* <http://www.tshaonline.org/ handbook/online/articles/ fbr41> [Accessed Feb. 27, 2015]; Joseph Milton Nance, "Mier Expedition," *The Handbook of Texas Online,* <http://www.tshaonline.org/handbook/online/articles/ qym02> [Accessed Feb. 27, 2015].

42. Anson Jones, *Memoranda and Official Correspondence Relating to the Republic of Texas* (New York: D. Appleton, 1859), 25 (quotation); Ephraim D. Adams, "Correspondence from the British Archives Concerning Texas, 1837–1845," *SHQ* 16 (July 1912): 77; David C. Humphrey, *Peg Leg: The Improbable Life of a Texas Hero, Thomas William Ward, 1807–1872* (Denton: Texas State Histori-

cal Association, 2009), 84–91; Haley, *Houston*, 252–253, 260–261; Siegel, *Political History*, 211–212; Claudia Hazlewood, "Archive War," *The Handbook of Texas Online*, <http://www.tshaonline.org/handbook/online/articles/mqa02> [Accessed Feb. 27, 2015].

43. Adams, "British Archives," 77, 127 (1st–3rd quotations); Jones, *Memoranda*, 256 (4th quotation); Wolfram M. Von-Maszewski (ed.), *Voyage to North America, 1844–1845: Prince Carl of Solms' Texas Diary of People, Places, and Events* (Denton: University of North Texas Press, 2000), 36 (5th quotation); Patsy M. Spaw (ed.), *The Texas Senate, Volume I: Republic to Civil War, 1836–1861* (College Station: Texas A&M University Press, 1991), 146; Siegel, *Political History*, 211–212; Moss, "Description," 15; "Hall, John W."

44. *National Vindicator* (Washington), Nov. 25, 1843; *Texas National Register* (Washington), May 15, 1845 *Daily Statesman* (Austin), Nov. 26, 1899; Lack, *Gray Diary*, 115; Gammel, *Laws of Texas*, I, 837; Wallis and Hill, *Lockhart*, 47; Kemp, *Signers*, xv; Moss, "Description," 16, Appendix: 11; Pennington, *Washington County*, 102; Eugene C. Barker, "Notes on Early Texas Newspapers, 1819–1836," *SHQ* (October 1917): 143; Douglas C. McMurtrie, "Pioneer Printing in Texas," *SHQ* (January 1932): 188; Marilyn M. Sibley, *Lone Stars and State Gazettes: Texas Newspapers Before the Civil War* (College Station: Texas A&M University Press, 1983), 135, 180–82 (quotation); Ferdinand D. Baillio, *History of the Texas Press Association* (Dallas: Southwestern Publishing Co., 1916), 330, 358–359; David Bebbington, *Victorian Religious Revivals: Culture and Piety in Local and Global Contexts* (Oxford, UK: Oxford University Press, 2012), 67; James L. Haley, "Gant, William Washington," *The Handbook of Texas Online*, <http://www.tshaonline.org/handbook/online/articles/fga15> [Accessed Mar. 2, 2015]; Carole E. Christian, "Texas Emigrant," *The Handbook of Texas Online*, <http://www.tshaonline.org/handbook/online/articles/eeto8> [Accessed Mar. 2, 2015]; "Miller, Washington D.," *The Handbook of Texas Online*, <http://www.tshaonline.org/handbook/online/articles/fmi29> [Accessed Mar. 2, 2015]; Vivian Elizabeth Smyrl, "Cushney, William H.," *The Handbook of Texas Online*, <http://www.tshaonline.org/handbook/online/articles/fcu39> [Accessed Mar. 2, 2015]; Carole E. Christian, "National Vindicator," *The Handbook of Texas Online*, <http://www.tshaonline.org/handbook/online/articles/eeno4> [Accessed Mar. 2, 2015]; Carole E. Christian, "Texas National Register," *The Handbook of Texas Online*, <http://www.tshaonline.org/handbook/online/articles/eeti3> [Accessed Mar. 2, 2015].

45. Austin *Daily Statesman*, Nov. 26, 1899; *Dallas Morning News*, July 23, 1905; Moore, *Savage Frontier, Volume IV*, 126–127; Siegel, *Big Men Walked Here*, 52–53; DeShields, *Border Wars of Texas*, 377–380; Anna Muckleroy, "The Indian Policy of the Republic of Texas," *SHQ* 26 (January 1923): 192–196; Christian, "Washington-on-the-Brazos."

46. *Dallas Morning News*, July 8, 1958, July 2, 1960, June 2, 1968, Apr. 9, 1973; J. K. Holland, "Reminiscences of Austin and Washington," *Quarterly of the Texas State Historical Association* 1 (October 1897): 93–94; Wallis and Hill, *Lockhart*, 56; Von-Maszewski, *Voyage*, 77; Morris Card Files; Moss, "Description," 3, 13–15, 17, 160, Appendix: 15; Haley, *Houston*, 253, 254, 275; Humphrey, *Peg Leg*, 96; Spaw, *Senate History*, 120; *Daughters of the Republic of Texas Patriot Ancestor Album* (Paducah, Ky.: Turner Publishing Co., 2001), 131.

47. *National Vindicator* (Washington), Dec. 16, 1843 (1st quotation); *Texas National Register* (Washington), Dec, 7, 1844, June 5, Sept. 4, 1845 (2nd quotation); Richard S. Hunt and Jesse S. Randal, *A New Guide to Texas* (New York: Sher-

man & Smith, 1846), 62; Moss, "Description," 13, 15–17, Appendix: 15.

48. *Telegraph and Texas Register* (Houston), Jan. 27, Nov. 2, 1837; *Houston Weekly Telegraph*, May 31, Oct. 11, 1843, Jan. 3, 1844; *National Vindicator* (Washington), Apr. 20, 1844; *Picayune* (New Orleans), Apr. 15, 1845; *Advocate* (Victoria), May 24, 1850; *Texas State Gazette* (Austin), Jan. 30, 1858; *Dallas Morning News*, Sept. 15, 1963; William R. Hogan, *The Texas Republic: A Social and Economic History* (Norman: University of Oklahoma Press, 1946), 55–56, 60; Thomas W. Cutrer, "Kendall, George Wilkins," *The Handbook of Texas Online*, <http://www.tshaonline.org/handbook/online/articles/fke19> [Accessed Mar. 2, 2015].

49. *Telegraph and Texas Register* (Houston), Oct. 18, Nov. 9 and 26, Dec. 22, 1836; Puryear and Winfield, *Sandbars and Sternwheelers*, 46–48; Muir, "Destiny of Buffalo Bayou," 103–104; Lois Wood Burkhalter, "Yellow Stone," *The Handbook of Texas Online*, <http://www.tshaonline.org/handbook/online/articles/ety01> [Accessed Mar. 2, 2015].

50. *Houston Weekly Telegraph*, Dec. 14, 1842, Feb. 1, 1843; *Texian and Brazos Farmer* (Washington), Feb. 28, 1843; *National Vindicator* (Washington), Nov. 25, 1843, *Telegraph and Texas Register* (Houston), Nov. 29, 1843; *Dallas Morning News*, Oct. 29, 1899; Wallis and Hill, *Lockhart*, 84–85; Puryear and Winfield, *Sandbars and Sternwheelers*, 55–57, 117.

51. *Telegraph and Texas Register* (Houston), May 4, 1842; *Houston Weekly Telegraph*, Dec. 27, 1843 (quotations); *National Vindicator* (Washington), Dec. 16, 1843, Jan. 13, 1844; *Texas National Register* (Washington), May 8 and 22, 1845; Puryear and Winfield, *Sandbars and Sternwheelers*, 57, 116.

52. *Texas National Register* (Washington), July 17, Aug. 14, 1845; *Northern Standard* (Clarksville), May 13, 1845 (1st quotation); Pennington, *Washington County*, 105 (2nd quotation); Siegel, *Political History*, 252–253; Kameron K. Searle, "Election Returns from Lake Creek Settlement," <http://texashistorypage.com/Election_Returns_from_Lake_Creek_Settlement.html> [Accessed Feb. 27, 2015]; C. T. Neu, "Annexation," *The Handbook of Texas Online*, <http://www.tshaonline.org/handbook/online/articles/mga02> [Accessed Feb. 27, 2015].

53. *Texas National Register* (Washington), Sept. 4, Oct. 2, 1845; Moore, *Savage Frontier, Vol. IV*, 171.

54. *Texas Democrat* (Austin), May 6, June 3 and 17, 1846, *Telegraph and Texas Register* (Houston), May 13 and 27, June 3, 1846; *Northern Standard* (Clarksville), April 8, 1847; Charles D. Spurlin (comp.), *Texas Veterans in the Mexican War* (Nacogdoches, Tex.: Ericson Books, 1984), 17, 25–27, 89, 99–102; Harold J. Weiss Jr., "Hays, John Coffee," *The Handbook of Texas Online*, <http://www.tshaonline.org/handbook/online/articles/fhabq> [Accessed Feb. 26, 2015].

Chapter 3: COMMERCIAL CENTER

55. *Dallas Morning News*, July 26, 1960, Feb. 28, 1970; Dietrich, *Blazing Story*, 162–163; Andrew F. Muir, "The Destiny of Buffalo Bayou," *SHQ* 47 (October 1943): 91–92.

56. *Northern Standard* (Clarksville), May 20, 1848; *Nacogdoches Chronicle*, Mar. 28, 1854; Puryear and Winfield, *Sandbars and Sternwheelers*, 18–19, 25–29.

57. *Texas Ranger and Lone Star* (Washington), May 26, June 9, Sept. 3, 1853, Sept. 8 and 15, 1854; *Standard* (Clarksville), June 16, 1855; Allen to Bertrand, July 1, 1855 (Star of the Republic Museum); Gammel, *Laws of Texas*, III, 571–576; Earl F. Woodward, "Internal Improvements in Texas in the Early 1850s," *SHQ* 76 (October 1972): 172–173; Muir, "Destiny of Buffalo Bayou," 105; David G. McComb,

Galveston: A History (Austin: University of Texas Press, 1986), 57; Puryear and Winfield, *Sandbars and Sternwheelers*, xviii, 20–25, 29; Leonard Kubiak, "History of Steamboats in Texas," <http://www.forttumbleweed.net/steamboats.html> [Accessed Mar. 3, 2015]; *Report of the Chief of Engineers, Part 4*, H. Doc. 2, 57th Cong. 2nd Sess., p. 2602 (Ser. 4,447); Lou Ellen Ruesink, "Taming the Brazos," *Texas Water Resources* 3 (Aug. 1977): 2; "Galveston and Brazos Navigation Company," *The Handbook of Texas Online*, <http://www.tshaonline.org/handbook/online/articles/dqg01> [Accessed Mar. 3, 2015].

58. *Houston Weekly Telegraph*, May 18, June 1, 1848; Wallis and Hill, *Lockhart*, 86; Puryear and Winfield, *Sandbars and Sternwheelers*, 60–62; Bryan, "Navigation of the Brazos River," 262.

59. *Northern Standard* (Clarksville), May 20, 1848; *Texas Ranger and Brazos Guard* (Washington), Jan. 16, 1849; *Dallas Morning News*, Oct. 29, 1899; Bryan, "Navigation of the Brazos River," 262–263; Puryear and Winfield, *Sandbars and Sternwheelers*, 18, 64; James C. Kearney, *Nassau Plantation: The Evolution of a Texas German Slave Plantation* (Denton: University of North Texas Press, 2011), 167 (quotation).

60. *Houston Weekly Telegraph*, Jan. 25, Mar. 15, Oct. 4, Nov. 1, 1849, Jan. 17, May 30, June 20, 1850; *Texas Ranger and Brazos Guard* (Washington), Mar. 9, 1849; *Galveston Weekly News*, Mar. 11, 1850; *Telegraph and Texas Register* (Houston), May 23, June 20, 1850; *Texas State Gazette* (Austin), May 25, 1850; Louis W. Kemp (ed.), "Early Days in Milam County: Reminiscences of Susan Turnham McCown," *SHQ* 50 (Jan. 1947): 373–374; Puryear and Winfield, *Sandbars and Sternwheelers*, 19, 15, 66–68, 115–116; Brockman, "Port Sullivan," chap. 2; Abigail C. Holbrook, "Cotton Marketing in Antebellum Texas," *SHQ* 50 (Apr. 1970): 448.

61. *Galveston Weekly News*, June 3 and 24, 1851; *Texas Ranger and Lone Star* (Washington), Mar. 25, Apr. 25, Dec. 15 and 29, 1853, Mar. 9, Apr. 6, June 22, Aug. 3, Nov. 9, 1854; *Dallas Morning News*, Oct. 29, 1899; Puryear and Winfield, *Sandbars and Sternwheelers*, 68–69, 116–118; Holbrook, "Cotton Marketing," 447–449; Brockman, "Port Sullivan," chap. 2; Bryan, "Navigation of the Brazos River," 262.

62. *Texas Ranger and Lone Star* (Washington), June 9, Oct. 22, Nov. 5 and 12, 1853, Jan. 1, 1854 (quotation), Feb. 23, 1856; *Washington American*, Apr. 30, Oct. 12, Dec. 3, 1856, Mar. 10 and 31, 1857; Martin Donell Kohout, "Stephenson, Hugh," *The Handbook of Texas Online*, <http://www.tshaonline.org/handbook/online/articles/fstcx> [Accessed Feb. 26, 2015].

63. *Houston Weekly Telegraph*, Jan. 17, June 20, 1850; *Semi-Weekly Star* (Washington), June 26, 1850 (quotation); *Texas State Gazette* (Austin), Mar. 27, 1852; *Lone Star and Southern Watch Tower* (Washington), May 15 and 29, 1852; *Weekly Journal* (Galveston), Mar. 19, Apr. 9, May 28, June 4, 1852; *Texas Ranger and Lone Star* (Washington), Mar. 13, Apr. 25, 1853, Jan. 12, 1854; *Galveston Weekly News*, Jan. 3, 1854; Puryear and Winfield, *Sandbars and Sidewheelers*, 70, 72–75, 115; Brockman, "Port Sullivan," chap. 2.

64. *Galveston Weekly News*, Mar. 19, May 28, 1852, Feb. 1, 1853; *Texas Ranger and Lone Star* (Washington), Nov. 20 and 27, 1852, Mar. 25, Dec. 15 and 29, 1853, Mar. 9, Apr. 6, May 4 and 11, 1854, May 24, 1855; *Telegraph and Texas Register* (Houston), Dec. 3, 1852; *Weekly Journal* (Galveston), Jan. 28, 1853; *Texas State Gazette* (Austin), Feb. 28, 1857; Puryear and Winfield, *Sandbars and Sternwheelers*, 75–78 (quotation), 117; Brockman, "Port Sullivan," chap. 2; Murphy Givens,

"Henry Kinney's Lone Star Fair Opened 160 Years Ago This Week," <http://www. caller.com/opinion/columnists/murphy-givens/henry-kinneys-lone-star-fair-opened-160-years> [Accessed Oct. 28, 2014]; Carole E. Christian, "William Penn, TX," *The Handbook of Texas Online*, <http://www.tshaonline.org/handbook/online/articles/ hlw36), [Accessed Mar. 3, 2015].

65. *Texas Ranger and Lone Star* (Washington), Mar. 25, 1853; Wallis and Hill, *Lockhart*, 86; Puryear and Winfield, *Sandbars and Sternwheelers*, 79–80; Carole E. Christian, "Warren, TX (Washington County)," *The Handbook of Texas Online*, <http://www.tshaonline.org/handbook/online/articles/hvw84> [Accessed Mar. 3, 2015].

66. *Texas Ranger and Lone Star* (Washington), Apr. 27, June 8, July 13, Oct. 5, 1854; *Standard* (Clarksville), May 29, 1854; *Nacogdoches Chronicle*, Oct. 10, 1854; Puryear and Winfield, *Sandbars and Sidewheelers*, 22, 83–84; Christian, "Warren, TX."

67. *Texas Ranger and Brazos Guard* (Washington), Jan. 16, 1849; *Semi-Weekly Star* (Washington), June 26, 1850; *Lone Star and Southern Watch Tower* (Washington), Apr. 5, 1851; *Nacogdoches Chronicle*, Sept. 11, Dec. 7, 1852, Mar. 15, 1853; *Texas Ranger and Lone Star* (Washington), Oct. 6, 1855 (quotation), Feb. 1, 1856; *Daily News* (Galveston), June 18, 1893; *Daily Statesman* (Austin), Nov. 26, 1899; Morris Card Files; Moss, "Description," 19–20, Appendix: 20; Sibley, *Lone Stars*, 252; Pennington, *Washington County*, 102–103; Hobart Huson, "Lancaster, Joseph," *The Handbook of Texas Online*, <http://www.tshaonline.org/handbook/ online/articles/fla19> [Accessed Feb. 27, 2015].

68. *Texas Ranger and Brazos Guard* (Washington), Jan. 16, 1849 (1st and 2nd quotations); "Bolivar" to A. R. McGuire, Oct. 5, 1849 (3rd quotation) (Star of the Republic Museum); Melinda Rankin, *Texas in 1850* (Boston: Damrell and Moore, 1852), 147 (4th quotation); Bryan, "Navigation of the Brazos River," 263.

69. *Weekly Journal* (Galveston), Aug. 6, 1852 (1st quotation); *Texas Ranger and Lone Star* (Washington), Oct. 6, 1852 (2nd and 5th quotations), Apr. 25, Oct. 15 (3rd quotation), Nov. 26, Dec. 15 and 29, 1853; *Texas State Gazette* (Austin), Apr. 4, 1854; *Daily News* (Galveston), Feb. 28, 1904 (4th quotation); Moss, "Description," 19, 20–22, Appendix: 21; Shuffler, "Signing," 319.

70. *Lone Star and Southern Watch Tower* (Washington), Apr. 5, 1851; *Texas Ranger and Lone Star* (Washington), Oct. 6, 1852; *Nacogdoches Chronicle*, July 26, 1853; *Washington American*, May 14, 21, and 28, 1856; *Proceedings of the Grand Lodge*, 233–234.

71. *Texas Ranger and Lone Star* (Washington), July 13 and 27, Aug. 17, 1854; *Texas State Gazette* (Austin), Sept. 2, 1854; *Washington American*, Apr. 2, May 14, 21, and 28, 1856, Feb. 10, June 2, 1857; Ernest W. Winkler, "Check List of Texas Imprints, 1846–1876," *SHQ* 48 (July 1944): 43 (quotation).

72. *Nacogdoches Chronicle*, Sept. 11, 1852; *Texas Ranger and Lone Star* (Washington), Apr. 1, 1853; *Washington American*, June 4, 1856; Smith to Peel, June 10, 1852 (1st quotation), Ruter Papers (CAH); Rankin, *Texas in 1850*, 148 (2nd quotation); Phelan, *Early Methodism*, 427; Cody, "Ruter," 33–34; Nath and Judy Winfield, "Felder, Gabriel," *The Handbook of Texas Online*, <http://www.tshaonline. org/handbook/online/articles/ffe13> [Accessed Mar. 7, 2015].

73. *Nacogdoches Chronicle*, Sept. 11, 1852; *Washington American*, Feb. 3, 1857; Morrell, *Flowers and Fruits*, 135; Rankin, *Texas in 1850*, 149; Morris Card Files; Moss, "Description," Appendix: 20; Baker, *Blossoming Desert*, 94; Joseph E. Early Jr., *A Texas Baptist History Sourcebook* (Denton: University of North Texas Press,

2004), 57, 74–77; Travis L. Summerlin, "Baylor, Robert Emmett Bledsoe," *The Handbook of Texas Online*, <http://www.tshaonline.org/handbook/online/articles/fbaav> [Accessed Mar. 7, 2015]; William J. Stone Jr., "Texas Baptist [1855–61]," *The Handbook of Texas Online*, <http://www.tshaonline.org/handbook/online/articles/ibto2> [Accessed Mar. 7, 2015].

74. *Nacogdoches Chronicle*, Sept. 11, 1852; William R. Lott, "Washington Presbyterian Church," (manuscript), Apr. 10, 1891 (quotation; Star of the Republic Museum); William S. Red (ed.), "Allen's Reminiscences of Texas, 1838–1842," *SHQ* 17 (Jan. 1914): 283–284; William S. Red, *A History of the Presbyterian Church in Texas* (Austin: Steck Co., 1936), 82, 101, 137, 141; Ernest W. Winkler, "Checklist of Texas Imprints, 1846–1876," *SHQ* 48 (January 1945): 384; W. L. Montague et al. (eds.), *Biographical Record of the Alumni of Amherst College* (Amherst, Mass.: J. E. Williams, 1883), 163; "Allen, William Youel," *The Handbook of Texas Online*, <http:// www.tshaonline.org/handbook/online/articles/fal30> [Accessed Mar. 8, 2015].

75. *Nacogdoches Chronicle*, Sept. 11, 1852; Morris Card Files; "St. Paul's Episcopal, Navasota, Texas," <http://www.stpaulsnavasota.org/history-st-pauls/> [Accessed Mar. 8, 2015]; "Stanford University Libraries: SearchWorks Catalog," <http://searchworks.stanford.edu/view/8131165> [Accessed Oct. 18, 2015]; Moss, "Description," 22–23, Appendix: 20; Dubose Murphy, "Early Days of the Protestant Episcopal Church in Texas," *SHQ* 34 (April 1931): 299, 310–311, 314; "Gillette, Charles," *The Handbook of Texas Online*, <http://www.tshaonline.org/handbook/online/articles/fgi28> [Accessed Mar. 8, 2015]; William James Battle, "Gregg, Alexander," *The Handbook of Texas Online*, <http://www.tshaonline.org/handbook/online/articles/fgr47> [Accessed Mar. 8, 2015].

76. *Texas Ranger and Lone Star* (Washington), June 8, 1854; Hogan, *Texas Republic*, 136–137; Grusendorf, "Education in Washington County," 259–263, 270; Evans, *Texas Schools*, 65–67; Max Berger and Lee Wilborn, "Education," *The Handbook of Texas Online*, <http://www. tshaonline.org/handbook/online/articles/kheo1> [Accessed Mar. 12, 2015].

77. *Lone Star and Southern Watch Tower* (Washington), Apr. 5, 1851, June 12, 1852; *Texas Ranger and Lone Star* (Washington), Mar. 11, 1853, June 29, 1854; *Proceedings of the Grand Lodge*, 233–234; "My Family: Lindsey Powell Rucker"; Grusendorf, "Education in Washington County," 234–236; James D. Carter, *Education and Masonry in Texas, 1846–1861* (Waco: Grand Lodge of Texas, 1964), 394–396; Samuel J. M. Eaton, *History of the Presbytery of Eaton* (New York: Hurd & Houghton, 1868), 336–339; Carole E. Christian, "Washington Masonic Academy," *The Handbook of Texas Online*, <http://www.tshaonline.org/handbook/online/articles/kbwo5> [Accessed Mar. 8, 2015].

78. *Texas Ranger and Lone Star* (Washington), Mar. 11, Apr. 25, June 16 and 23, Oct. 15, 1853, Jan. 26, June 29, 1854, Feb. 10, Apr. 21, May 24, July 14, Dec. 22, 1855, Jan. 5, 1856; "My Family: Lindsey Powell Rucker"; Carter, *Education and Masonry*, 396–397; Grusendorf, "Education in Washington County," 236–238.

79. *Texas National Register* (Washington), Feb. 15, 1845; *Texas Ranger and Lone Star* (Washington), Apr. 21, May 24, 1855; *Washington American*, Oct. 29, Nov. 5 and 12, 1856; *Dallas Morning News*, June 19, 1930; Eby, *Source Book*, 400; Jack W. Humphries, "The Law Department at Old Austin College," *SHQ* 83 (April 1980): 373; Robert F. Miller, "Early Presbyterianism in Texas as Seen by Rev. James Weston Miller, D.D.," *SHQ* 19 (October 1915): 167–168, 172; Red, *Presbyterian Church*, 230; Grusendorf, "Education in Washington County," 238; J. D.

Fuller, "Austin College," *The Handbook of Texas Online,* <http://www.tshaonline.org/handbook/online/articles/kba15> [Accessed Mar. 8, 2015]; Lillie M. Russell and Lois Smith Murray, "Baylor University," *The Handbook of Texas Online,* <http://www.tshaonline.org/handbook/online/articles/kbb05> [Accessed Mar. 8, 2015]; Carole E. Christian, "Soule University," *The Handbook of Texas Online,* <http://www.tshaonline.org/handbook/online/articles/kbs24> [Accessed Mar. 8, 2015].

80. *Texas Ranger and Lone Star* (Washington), Jan. 19 and 26 (quotation), 1856; *Washington American,* Apr. 23, 1856, Mar. 10, Jul. 21, 1857; *Texas Ranger and Lone Star* (Brenham), Apr. 29, 1857; Morris Card Files; Gammel, *Laws of Texas,* V, 297; Eby, *Source Book,* 399; *Papers in the Case of Giddings vs. Clark, Third Congressional District of Texas,* H. Misc. Doc. 163, 42nd Cong., 2nd Sess., 1871–1872 (Ser. 1,526), 27; Stephen A. Hodgman, *The Nation's Sin and Punishment* (New York: Doolady, 1864), passim; Carter, *Education and Masonry,* 372–373.

81. *Texas Ranger and Brazos Guard* (Washington), Oct. 19, 1849 (2nd quotation); *Nacogdoches Chronicle,* Mar. 21, 1854; *Texas Ranger and Lone Star* (Washington), Feb. 26, 1854, June 23, 1855; *Washington American,* Feb. 8, Apr. 2, May 14, 21, and 28, 1856; *Houston Weekly Telegraph,* Aug. 25, 1858; *San Antonio Ledger & Texan,* Sept. 11, 1858; Roger Conger, "An 1849 R. M. Williamson Letter," *SHQ* 65 (April 1962): 398 (1st quotation); Sibley, *Lone Stars,* 180; Pennington, *Washington County,* 103.

82. *Texas Ranger and Lone Star* (Washington), Mar. 30, June 22, 1854; *Texas State Gazette* (Austin), Apr. 4, July 13, Oct. 7 and 21, 1854; Dudley G. Wooten (ed.), *A Comprehensive History of Texas and Texans, 1865 to 1897,* 2 vols. (Dallas: William G. Scarff, 1898), II, 607; McCaslin, *Fighting Stock,* 54, 56; T. Michael Parrish, "Rogers, William Peleg," *The Handbook of Texas Online,* <http://www.tshaonline.org/handbook/online/articles/fro64> [Accessed Mar. 8, 2015].

83. *Lone Star and Southern Watch Tower* (Washington), Apr. 5, 1851; *Texas Ranger and Lone Star* (Washington), Aug. 3 and 10, 1854; *Washington American,* June 11, 18, and 25, July 9, Nov. 19, Dec. 30, 1856; Gammel, *Laws of Texas,* V, 297; *Proceedings of the Grand Lodge,* 216.

84. *Houston Weekly Telegraph,* Apr. 27, 1848; *Weekly Journal* (Galveston), Oct. 1, 1852; *Texas Ranger and Lone Star* (Washington), Apr. 25, June 16 and 23, 1853; *San Antonio Ledger & Texan,* July 7, 1853; Ernest W. Winkler (ed.), "Platforms of Political Parties in Texas," *Bulletin of the University of Texas* 53 (Sept. 20, 1916): 54–55; Paul M. Lucko, "Prison System," *The Handbook of Texas Online,* <http://www.tshaonline.org/handbook/online/articles/jjp03> [Accessed Feb. 27, 2015].

85. *Lone Star and Southern Watch Tower* (Washington), Apr. 5, 1851 (2nd and 3rd quotations); *Texas Ranger and Lone Star* (Washington), Oct. 15 (1st quotation), Nov. 26, 1853, Feb. 2, 1854 (4th quotation); *Washington American,* Mar. 7, (5th quotation), June 11, 1856; Gammel, *Laws of Texas,* III, 1152–1154.

86. *Weekly Journal* (Galveston), July 9 and 16, 1852; *Texas Ranger and Lone Star* (Washington), Apr. 6, 20, and 27, Oct. 19, Nov. 18, 1854; *Texas State Gazette* (Austin), Apr. 15 and 22, 1854; *San Antonio Ledger & Texan,* Sept. 11, 1858; *Houston Weekly Telegraph,* Aug. 25, 1858; *Proceedings of the Grand Lodge,* 579–580; Carl H. Moneyhon, "Landholding in Brazos County, Texas: Frontier, War, and Reconstruction," *This Corner of Canaan: Essays on Texas in Honor of Randolph B. Campbell,* ed. Richard B. McCaslin, Donald E. Chipman, and Andrew J. Torget (Denton: University of North Texas Press, 2013), 152.

87. *Weekly Journal* (Galveston), Apr. 2, 1852; *Dallas Morning News,* Feb. 21, 1900; *Houston Post,* Apr. 29, 1900; Sue Owens, "James Walker Sr.," http://archiver.

rootsweb.ancestry.com/th/read/WALKER/1997-12/0881396953> [Accessed Mar. 3, 2015]; Johnson, "Walker, James."

88. *Texas Ranger and Lone Star* (Washington), Aug. 10 and 24, Sept. 8, 1854; Gammel, *Laws of Texas,* III, 1305; Brown, *Indian Wars and Pioneers of Texas,* 430; "Find a Grave: Robert Alexander Lott."

89. *Texas Ranger and Lone Star* (Washington), Oct. 6, 1852, Oct. 15, Nov. 26, 1853; *Texas State Gazette* (Austin), Apr. 4, 1854 (quotation); Moss, "Description," 22–23.

Chapter 4: ERA OF CONFLICT

90. *Texas Ranger and Lone Star* (Washington), Nov. 9, 1854, Mar. 10 and 17, Sept. 8, 1855, Feb 2, 1856; *Washington American,* Feb. 1 and 15, 1856; *Texas State Gazette* (Austin), Mar. 3, May 5, 1855; *Dallas Morning News,* Oct. 29, 1899; *Reports of Cases Argued and Decided in the Supreme Court of the State of Texas* (St. Louis: Gilbert Book Co., 1882), XXIX, 221*ff*; John M. Brockman, "Port Sullivan: Ghost Town" (M.A. thesis, Texas A&M University, 1968), chap. 3, <http://www.rootsweb.ancestry.com/~txrober2/books/PortSullivanIII.htm> [Accessed Mar. 3, 2015]; Bryan, "Navigation of the Brazos River," 262; Pennington, *Washington County,* 104; Puryear and Winfield, *Sandbars and Sternwheelers,* 85–87, 116; Christian, "Warren, TX."

91. *Washington American,* Mar. 19, 1856; *Houston Weekly Telegraph,* July 14, Nov. 10, 1858, May 18, June 8, 1859; *Southern Beacon* (Henderson), Jan. 22, 1859; Watson, "Diary," 42; Puryear and Winfield, *Sandbars and Sternwheelers,* 89–91.

92. *Texas Ranger and Lone Star* (Washington), Sept. 17, 1853, Apr. 27, 1854; *Texas Almanac for 1857,* 82; H. Bailey Carroll, "Texas Collection," *SHQ* 49 (July 1945): 146–147; Woodward, "Internal Improvements," 173–177; George C. Werner, "Buffalo Bayou, Brazos And Colorado Railway," *The Handbook of Texas Online,* <http://www.tshaonline.org/handbook/online/articles/eqb16)> [Accessed Mar. 12, 2015]; Thomas W. Cutrer, "Heard, Thomas Jefferson," *The Handbook of Texas Online,* <http://www.tshaonline.org/handbook/online/articles/ fhe03> [Accessed Mar. 12, 2015].

93. *Texas Ranger and Lone Star* (Washington), Sept. 3, 1853, Dec. 8, 1855; *Texas State Gazette* (Austin), Sept. 10 and 24, 1853, Jan. 20, 1855 (1st quotation); *Washington American,* Dec. 7, 1855; *Daily Statesman* (Austin), Nov. 26, 1899; *Dallas Morning News,* Sept. 18, 1921 (2nd quotation); Woodward, "Internal Improvements," 178–179; Pennington, *Washington County,* 104–105; "Find a Grave: Kathleen Emma *Crawford* Randle," <http://www.findagrave.com/cgi-bin/fg.cgi?page=gr&GRid=44834851> [Accessed Mar. 12, 2015]; Nancy Beck Young, "Galveston And Red River Railroad," *The Handbook of Texas Online,* <http://www.tshaonline.org/handbook/ online/articles/eqg02> [Accessed Mar. 12, 2015]; George C. Werner, "Houston and Texas Central Railway," *The Handbook of Texas Online,* <http://www.tshaonline.org/handbook/online/articles/eqh09> [Accessed Mar. 12, 2015].

94. *Houston Weekly Telegraph,* July 14, 1858 (1st quotation); *Dallas Morning News,* June 13 (2nd quotation), Oct. 29, 1899; Bryan, "Navigation of the Brazos River," 262.

95. *Washington American,* Nov. 19, 1856, Jan. 27, Feb. 3, 10, 17, and 24, Aug. 4, 11, and 18 (quotations), 1857; Gammel, *Laws of Texas,* IV, 121–125.

96. *Texas State Gazette* (Austin), Apr. 30, 1859; *Houston Tri-Weekly Telegraph,* Dec. 1 and 4, 1860; *Brenham Weekly Banner,* July 18, Aug. 1, Sept. 12, 19, and 26, Oct. 3, 1879; *Daily Statesman* (Austin), Nov. 26, 1899; *Brenham Daily Press,* Sept.

1, 1913; Gammel, *Laws of Texas,* V, 1443; S. G. Reed, "Central and Montgomery Railway," *The Handbook of Texas Online,* <http://www.tshaonline.org/handbook/online/articles/eqc04> [Accessed Mar. 12, 2015]; Carole E. Christian, "Washington County Rail Road," *The Handbook of Texas Online,* <http://www.tshaonline.org/handbook/online/articles/eqw06> [Accessed Mar. 12, 2015].

97. *Texas Ranger and Lone Star* (Washington), Dec. 15 and 29, 1853, Jan. 23, Feb. 24 (1st quotation), Apr. 21, 1855 (2nd quotation), Feb. 16, 1856; *Washington American,* Nov. 1 and 30, 1855, Feb. 1, July 23, Oct. 8, 1856; Morris Card File.

98. *Texas State Gazette* (Austin), June 23 and 30, 1855; *Texas Ranger and Lone Star* (Washington), July 21 and 28, Aug. 2, 1855; Carol M. Allen to John R. Bertrand, July 1 and 24, 1855 (Star of the Republic Museum); Llerena B. Friend, "Additional Items for the Winkler Checklist of Texas Imprints, 1846–1860," *SHQ* 65 (October 1961): 104; Ralph Wooster, "An Analysis of the Texas Know Nothings," *SHQ* 70 (January 1967): 414, 417, 419; Winkler, *Political Parties in Texas,* 63; Duncan W. Robinson, *Judge Robert McAlpin Williamson* (Austin: Texas State Historical Association, 1948), 212–213.

99. *Texas Ranger and Lone Star* (Washington), June 23, July 28, Aug. 11, 1855; *Standard* (Clarksville), Sept. 3, 1855; *Texas Ranger and Lone Star* (Brenham), Aug. 29, 1857; Morris Card Files; Allen to Bertrand, July 24, 1855 (Star of the Republic Museum); Wooster, "Texas Know Nothings," 415–416; Alma D. King, "The Political Career of William Simpson Oldham," *SHQ* 33 (October 1929): 117–118; "Texas Legislators, Past & Present: John Sayles," <http://www.lrl.state.tx.us/legeLeaders/members/membersearch.cfm> [Accessed Mar. 2, 2015].

100. *Huntsville Item,* Jan. 5, 1856 (quotation); *Washington American,* July 30, Aug. 6 and 20 (quotation), Oct. 1, 8, 15, 22, and 29, Nov.12, 1856; *Texas State Gazette* (Austin), Oct. 11, 1856; Allen to Bertrand, July 24, 1855 (Star of the Republic Museum); Wooster, "Texas Know Nothings," 415–417.

101. *Washington American,* July 30, 1856; *Texas State Gazette* (Austin), Apr. 12, 1856; Jones, *Memoranda,* 549 (1st quotation), 551 (2nd and 3rd quotations), 552 (4th quotation).

102. *Texas Ranger and Lone Star* (Washington), Oct. 1, 1853, Jan. 22 (1st quotation), Aug. 18 (2nd–4th quotations), Oct. 6, 1855; *Texas State Gazette* (Austin), July 26, 1856; *Standard* (Clarksville), Aug. 16, 1856; *Cherokee Sentinel* (Rusk), Dec. 20, 1856.

103. *Semi-Weekly Star* (Washington), June 26, 1850; *Washington American,* Nov. 1, 1855, June 11, Nov. 19, 1856, Apr. 11, 1857; Morris Card Files; Sibley, *Lone Stars,* 252–253; Baillio, *Texas Press Association,* 359; Jennifer Eckel, "Crawford, George W.," *The Handbook of Texas Online,* <http://www.tshaonline.org/handbook/online/articles/fcr96> [Accessed Feb. 27, 2015].

104. *Washington American,* June 25, July 9, 1856.

105. *Washington American,* Sept. 10, 17, and 24 (quotations), Dec. 3, 1856; Harvey Wish, "The Slave Insurrection Panic of 1856," *Journal of Southern History* 5 (May 1939): 206–222; James M. Smallwood, "Slave Insurrections," *The Handbook of Texas Online,* <http://www.tshaonline.org/handbook/online/articles/jcs02> [Accessed Mar. 3, 2015].

106. *Washington American,* Feb. 3 and 17, 1857.

107. *Nacogdoches Chronicle* , Dec. 7, 1852; *Texas Ranger and Lone Star* (Washington), Aug. 24, Nov. 23, 1854, Feb. 1, 1856; *Washington American,* Mar. 7, June 11, 1856; *Texas State Gazette* (Austin), Mar. 26, 1859 (quotations).

108. *Washington American,* Nov. 12, 1856 (quotation); Sibley, *Lone Stars,* 253.

109. *Washington American*, July 9, Aug. 6, Nov. 19, Dec. 3 and 17, 1856, Jan. 27, Feb. 17, 1857; *Texas State Gazette* (Austin), Feb. 7, 1857; Pleasant B. Watson, "Diary" (typescript), 1858–1869, pp. 3–9 (Star of the Republic Museum); James C. Jamison, *With Walker in Nicaragua* (Columbia, Mo.: E. W. Stephenson Publishing Co., 1909), 138–141.

110. *Washington American*, Nov. 26, 1856 (1st quotation), Feb. 3, 10 and 17 (4th–6th quotations), Mar. 10, 1857; *Texas State Gazette* (Austin), Nov. 29, 1856, Feb. 7, 1857 (2nd and 3rd quotations); Wooster, "Texas Know Nothings," 418–421.

111. *Cherokee Sentinel* (Rusk), Jan. 17, 1857; *Texas Ranger and Lone Star* (Brenham), Aug. 29, 1857; *San Antonio Ledger & Texan*, May 22, Sept. 11, 1858; *Southern Intelligencer* (Austin), Aug. 11, 1858; *Houston Weekly Telegraph*, Sept. 28, 1859; *Texas State Gazette* (Austin), Oct. 1, 1859; *Flake's Bulletin* (Galveston), June 23, 1869; *Standard* (Clarksville), Oct. 15, 1869; Sibley, *Lone Stars*, 253.

112. *Houston Tri-Weekly Telegraph*, Sept. 22, 1860 (1st quotation); *Texas State Gazette* (Austin), Sept. 29, 1860 (2nd quotation); *Southern Intelligencer* (Austin), Oct. 10, 1860; *Navarro* (Tex.) *Express*, Nov. 2, 1860; Frank H. Smyrl, "Unionism in Texas, 1856–1861," *SHQ* 68 (October 1964): 180–182.

113. *Texas Ranger and Lone Star* (Brenham), Dec. 17, 1860; *Texas State Gazette* (Austin), Dec. 19, 1860; Sidney S. Johnson, *Texans Who Wore the Gray* (Tyler, Tex.: privately published, 1907), 87; Thomas W. Cutrer, "Oldham, Williamson Simpson," *The Handbook of Texas Online*, <http://www.tshaonline.org/handbook/online/articles/folo2> [Accessed Mar. 8, 2015]; Maberry, "Robertson, Jerome Bonaparte"; Robert Maberry Jr., "Robertson, Felix Huston," *The Handbook of Texas Online*, <http://www. tshaonline.org/handbook/online/articles/fro26> [Accessed Mar. 8, 2015]; Jennifer Eckel, "Shepard, James E.," *The Handbook of Texas Online*, <http://www.tshaonline.org/handbook/online/articles/fsh69> [Accessed Mar. 8, 2015].

114. *Texas Ranger and Lone Star* (Brenham), Dec. 17, 1860, *Texas State Gazette* (Austin), Dec. 19, 1860; Wallis and Hill, *Lockhart*, 34; Johnson, *Texans Who Wore the Gray*, 87; Stephen Chicoine, *Confederates of Chappell Hill, Texas: Prosperity, Civil War and Decline* (Jefferson, N.C.: McFarland & Co., 2004), 4; Frank W. Johnson, *A History of Texas and Texans*, 5 vols. (Chicago: American Historical Society, 1914), III, 1299–1300; Maberry, "Robertson, Jerome Bonaparte."

115. *Texas National Register* (Washington), June 6, 1845; *Lone Star and Southern Watch Tower* (Washington), Apr. 5, 1851; *Houston Tri-Weekly Telegraph*, Dec. 26, 1862; Joseph B. Polley, *A Soldier's Letters to Charming Nellie*, ed. Richard B. McCaslin (Knoxville: University of Tennessee Press, 2008), 38–39, 193, 195, 259; Stephen Chicoine (ed.), "Willing Never to Go Into Another Fight: The Civil War Correspondence of Rufus King Felder of Chappell Hill," *SHQ* 106 (April 2003): 577, 579; Harold B. Simpson (ed.), *Touched with Valor: Civil War Papers and Casualty Reports of Hood's Texas Brigade* (Hillsboro, Tex.: Hill Junior College Press, 1964), 86–88; Harold B. Simpson, *Hood's Texas Brigade: A Compendium* (Hillsboro, Tex.: Hill Junior College Press, 1977), 204–210; "Find a Grave: Walter Nathaniel Norwood," <http://www.findagrave.com/cgi-bin/fg.cgi?page=gr&GRid=28454706> [Accessed Mar. 8, 2015].

116. Polley, *Soldier's Letters*, 50–51; Chicoine, "Felder Correspondence," 579–580; Watson, "Diary," 77–99; Chicoine, *Confederates of Chappell Hill*, 50; Simpson, *Touched with Valor*, 89; Simpson, *Compendium*, 204–210.

117. Chicoine, "Felder Correspondence," 582; Simpson, *Touched with Valor*, 91; Simpson, *Compendium*, 204–210.

118. Chicoine, "Felder Correspondence," 585–86; Simpson, *Touched with Valor*, 92, 94, 96–97; Simpson, *Compendium*, 204–210; Maberry, "Robertson, Jerome Bonaparte."

119. Polley, *Soldier's Letters*, 146–147, 300–301;Chicoine, "Felder Correspondence," 589; Simpson, *Touched with Valor*, 95; Simpson, *Compendium*, 204–210.

120. Chicoine, "Felder Correspondence," 590 (quotation); Simpson, *Compendium*, 204–210.

121. *Houston Tri-Weekly Telegraph*, July 22, 1864; Watson, "Diary," 101–104; U.S. Department of War, Compiled Service Records of Confederate Soldiers Who Served in Organizations from Texas, RG 109, Benavides Cavalry: Pleasant B. Watson (National Archives); Simpson, *Compendium*, 204.

122. *Standard* (Clarksville), May 4, 1861; *Houston Tri-Weekly Telegraph*, Oct. 28, 1863, Apr. 15, 1864; *Flake's Bulletin* (Galveston), June 23, 1869; *Journal of the House of Representatives, Eighth Legislature* (Austin: John Marshall, 1860), 726; James M. Day (ed.), *House Journal of the Ninth Legislature, Regular Session of the State of Texas* (Austin: Texas State Library, 1964), 3; Archie Colburn, "Upson County Ga. Archives Biographies: Thomas Flewellen, 1799–1889," <http://files.usgwarchives.net/ga/upson/bios/gbs674flewelle.txt> [Accessed Mar. 8, 2015]; Louis W. Kemp, "Flewellen, Robert Turner," *The Handbook of Texas Online*, <http://www.tshaonline.org/handbook/online/articles/ffl11> [Accessed Mar. 8, 2015]; "Texas Legislators, Past & Present: Robert Flewellen," <http://www.lrl.state.tx.us/legeLeaders/members/membersearch.cfm> [Accessed Mar. 8, 2015]; Daniel F. Lisarelli, *The Last Prison: The Untold Story of Camp Groce CSA* (Boca Raton, Fla.: Universal Publishers, 1999), 37–38; McCaslin, *Fighting Stock*, 141.

123. *Houston Tri-Weekly Telegraph*, Jan. 8 and 19, 1864; Pennington, *Washington County*, 33.

124. *Houston Tri-Weekly Telegraph*, Feb. 16 (4th quotation), Mar. 13, 18 (3rd quotation), 23 (1st and 2nd quotations), May 6, 1863, Dec. 19, 1864; Compiled Service Records of Texas Confederate Soldiers, 2nd Texas Cavalry: Francis Lancaster, 24th Texas Cavalry: William Lancaster.

125. *Houston Tri-Weekly Telegraph*, Dec. 9, 1863; *Daily Statesman* (Austin), Nov. 26, 1899; *Dallas Morning News*, Feb. 28, 1970; Washington Citizens to John B. Magruder, [ca. Jan. 22, 1863], Texas Governor's Office, Papers: Francis R. Lubbock Papers (Archives Division, Texas State Library, Austin; cited hereafter as TSLA); Phelan, *Early Methodism*, 428; Bryan, "Navigation of the Brazos River," 264; Sue Winton Moss, "Historical Summary of the Town of Washington," *Report on the 1995 Archaeological and Historical Investigations at Washington-on-the-Brazos State Historical Park (41WT5), Washington County, Texas*, ed. David D. Kuehn, Technical Report No. 2 (College Station: Center for Environmental Archaeology, Texas A&M University, 1996), 17–20, 23, 24; E. Mott Davis and James E. Corbin, *Archeological Investigations at Washington-on-the-Brazos State Park*, Report No. 5 (Austin: Texas State Building Commission Archeological Program, 1967), 3.

126. *Houston Tri-Weekly Telegraph*, Dec. 4, 1862, Mar. 18, 1863, Aug. 31, 1864, Mar. 10, 1865; 263–267, 270, 273; Jim Wheat, "Postmasters & Post Offices of Texas, 1846–1930: Washington County," <http://www.rootsweb.ancestry.com/~txpost/washington.html> [Accessed Mar. 12, 2015]; "St. Paul's Episcopal, Navasota, Texas," <http://www.stpaulsnavasota.org/history-st-pauls/> [Accessed Mar. 12, 2015]; Grusendorf, "Education in Washington County."

Chapter 5: SHADOW TOWN

127. Dietrich, *Blazing Story*, 162–163.

128. Watson, "Diary," 104–109.

129. Donald G. Nieman, "African Americans and the Meaning of Freedom: Washington County, Texas as a Case Study, 1865–1886," *Chicago-Kent Law Review* 70 (January 1994): 551, 556; "Texas Legislators, Past & Present: Peter Diller," <http://www.lrl.state.tx.us/legeLeaders/members/membersearch.cfm> [Accessed Mar. 8, 2015]; Paul M. Lucko, "Watrous, Benjamin O.," *The Handbook of Texas Online*, <http://www.tshaonline.org/handbook/online/articles/fwaar> [Accessed Mar. 8, 2015].

130. *Houston Weekly Telegraph*, Aug. 25, 1858; *San Antonio Ledger & Texan*, Sept. 11, 1858; *Flake's Bulletin* (Galveston), July 19, 1867; Watson, "Diary," 112–114; Compiled Service Records for Texas Confederate Soldiers, 5th Texas Infantry: John W. Gee, Felix Farquhar; United States Eighth Census (1860), Washington County, Texas, Schedule 1 (Free Population): John Watson (National Archives); *Communication from Governor Pease of Texas, Relative to the Troubles in that State, May 11, 1868*, H. Misc. Doc. 127, 40th Cong., 2nd Sess., 1868 (Ser. 1,350), 8, 17; Nieman, "African Americans and the Meaning of Freedom," 551–552; Simpson, *Compendium*, 206.

131. *Flake's Bulletin* (Galveston), July 19, 1867; *San Antonio Express*, July 24, 1867; Watson, "Diary," 112–114; Nieman, "African Americans and the Meaning of Freedom," 551–552.

132. *Flake's Bulletin* (Galveston), Dec. 1 and 4, 1867; Watson, "Diary," 112–114 (quotation).

133. *Brenham Weekly Banner*, June 27, 1879; *Dallas Morning News*, Oct. 13, 1909; Watson, "Diary," 118–119 (quotation), 120; Dunn, "Farquhar Cemetery, Washington County."

134. *Houston Tri-Weekly Telegraph*, Sept. 22, 1863, July 18, 1871; *Flake's Bulletin* (Galveston), July 17 and 18, 1868; *Texas Countryman* (Hempstead), July 22, 1868; *New York Times*, July 25, 1868; *Daily Austin Republican*, Oct. 22, 1868; *Houston Daily Union*, Mar. 7, Aug. 18 and 21, 1871; *Galveston Tri-Weekly News*, July 28, 1871; *San Antonio Express*, July 22, 1871; "Texas Adjutant General Service Records for F. B. Lancaster," <http://www.tsl.state.tx.us/arc/service/index.php> [Accessed Mar. 11, 2015]; Christopher B. Bean, "A Stranger Among Strangers: An Analysis of the Freedmen's Bureau Sub-assistant Commissioners in Texas, 1865–1868" (Ph.D. diss., 2008, University of North Texas), 391–392; Mark Odintz, "Brazos County," *The Handbook of Texas Online*, <http://www.tshaonline.org/handbook/online/articles/hcb13> [Accessed Mar. 11, 2015].

135. *Houston Daily Union*, Feb. 8, 1869; *The Texas Almanac for 1867* (Galveston: W. Richardson & Co., 1866), 171–72; Nieman, "African Americans and the Meaning of Freedom," 544, 552–554; Terry Jordan, *German Seed in Texas Soil: Immigrant Farmers in Nineteenth-century Texas* (Austin: University of Texas Press, 1966), 52–53, 95, 116; Schmidt, *Washington County*, 23.

136. *Houston Daily Union*, Sept. 20, 1870 (1st quotation); *Brenham Weekly Banner*, June 21 (2nd quotation), Aug. 31, Nov. 22 and 29, 1878; Nieman, "African Americans and the Meaning of Freedom," 559–560, 564; Paul M. Lucko, "Guy, Bedford G.," *The Handbook of Texas Online*, <http://www.tshaonline.org/handbook/online/articles/fgupv> [Accessed Mar. 12, 2015]; Daniel J. Nabors, "Sledge,

Alonzo L.," *The Handbook of Texas Online*, <http://www.tshaonline.org/hand-book/online/articles/fsl06> [Accessed Mar. 12, 2015].

137. *New York Times*, Feb. 23, 1887; *Testimony on the Alleged Election Out-rages in Texas*, S. Misc. Doc. 62, 50th Cong., 2nd Sess. (Ser. 2,616), 12, 85–86, 157, 217, 321, 668–672; Nieman, "African Americans and the Meaning of Freedom," 561–562, 576–577; Robert W. Shook, "The Texas 'Election Outrage' of 1886," *East Texas Historical Journal* 10 (Spring 1972): 20–22; Thad Sitton and James H. Conrad, *Freedom Colonies: Independent Black Texans in the Time of Jim Crow* (Austin: University of Texas Press, 2005), 198; Carole E. Christian, "Lott, TX (Washington County)," *The Handbook of Texas Online*, <http://www.tshaonline. org/handbook/online/articles/ hvlar> [Accessed Mar. 12, 2015]; Carole E. Christian, "Graball, TX," *The Handbook of Texas Online*, <http://www.tshaonline.org/hand-book/online/articles/hrg24> [Accessed Mar. 12, 2015].

138. Shook, "Election Outrage," 22–23; Nieman, "African Americans and the Meaning of Freedom," 576–578; *Testimony on the Alleged Election Outrages*, 2–3.

139. *Brenham Weekly Banner*, Nov. 22, 1878; Shook, "Election Outrage," 20–24; Sitton and Conrad, *Freedom Colonies*, 154 (quotation); Paul M. Lucko, "Moore, R. J.," *The Handbook of Texas Online*, <http://www.tshaonline.org/hand-book/online/articles/fmoam> [Accessed Mar. 12, 2015]; "Texas Legislators, Past & Present: Robert J. Moore," <http://www.lrl.state.tx.us/legeLeaders/members/mem-bersearch.cfm> [Accessed Mar. 12, 2015].

140. *Brenham Weekly Banner*, Nov. 22, 1878, Jan. 9, Feb. 13, Nov. 13, 1890, Nov. 18, 1897; Wheat, "Postmasters & Post Offices of Texas, 1846–1930: Wash-ington County."

141. *Galveston Tri-Weekly News*, June 23, 1869; *Flake's Bulletin* (Galveston), June 23, 1869; *Dallas Weekly Herald*, July 10, 1869; *Dallas Morning News*, Nov. 30, 1895; Dietrich, *Blazing Story*, 182.

142. *Daily Austin Republican*, Aug. 26, 1868; *Flake's Bulletin* (Galveston), Aug. 27, 1868; *Galveston Tri-Weekly News,* Aug. 15, 1870; *Houston Daily Union*, Mar. 17, 1871, June 10, 1871 (quotation); *Dallas Weekly Herald*, Nov. 3, 1877; *Brenham Weekly Banner*, Oct. 18, 1878, July18, Aug. 1, Sept. 12, 19, and 26, Oct. 3, 1879; *Daily Statesman* (Austin), Nov. 26, 1899; *Brenham Daily Banner-Press*, Sept. 1, 1913; *Houston Post*, Apr. 29, 1900; *Dallas Morning News*, Feb. 3, 1929; *Texas State Gazetteer and Business Directory, 1884* (Chicago: R. L. Polk & Co., 1884), 712; Gammel, *Laws of Texas*, V, 1443, VI, 53–54, 1183–1184, 1346–1347, 1600–1601; Brown, *Indian Wars and Pioneers of Texas*, 497–498; Pennington, *Washington County,*100; "A Guide to the Angelina Smith Letters, 1842–1843," <http://www. lib.utexas.edu/taro/utcah/02374/cah-02374.html> [Accessed Mar. 12, 2015]; S. G. Reed, "Central and Montgomery Railway," *The Handbook of Texas Online*, <http:// www.tshaonline.org/handbook/online/articles/eqc04> [Accessed May 21, 2015].

143. *Dallas Morning News*, July 4 and 11, Oct. 29, 1899 (1st quotation), Nov. 30, 1900, June 23, 1909, Feb. 3, 1929; *Brenham Daily Banner-Press*, Dec. 10, 1913, Feb. 11, April 22, 1914; Bryan, "Navigation of the Brazos River," 265; Nan T. Ledbetter, "The Muddy Brazos in Early Texas History," *SHQ* 63 (October 1959): 238–239 (2nd quotation); Kenna Lang Archer, *Unruly Waters: A Social and Envi-ronmental History of the Brazos River* (Albuquerque: University of New Mexico Press, 2015), 70–72; Puryear and Winfield, *Sandbars and Sternwheelers*, 30–33.

144. *Galveston Weekly News*, Mar. 3, 1881 (quotation); *Dallas Morning News*, July 26, 1960, Feb. 28, 1970, Feb. 1, 1971; Morris Card Files; United States Tenth

Census (1880), Washington County, Texas, Enumeration District 139 (June 3, 1880), Schedule 1 (Population), Record Group 29 (National Archives, Washington, D.C); E. H. Loughery, *Texas State Government: A Volume of Biographical Sketches and Passing Comment* (Austin: McLeod & Jackson, 1897), 51–52; "Neal, George D.," *The Handbook of Texas Online*, <http://www.tshaonline.org/handbook/online/articles/fneo1> [Accessed Mar. 12, 2015].

145. *Flake's Bulletin* (Galveston), June 16, 1869; *Brenham Weekly Banner*, Nov. 22, 1878, Mar. 9, 1882, May 22, 1884; *Iola* (Kan.) *Register*, Feb. 3, 1882; *Galveston Weekly News*, Feb. 9, 1882; *Texas State Gazetteer and Business Directory, 1884*, 712; *Texas State Gazetteer and Business Directory, 1890–1891* (Chicago: R. L. Polk & Co., 1890), 1029; *Biennial Report of the Secretary of State of the State of Texas* (Austin: State Printing Office, 1882), 20.

146. *Brenham Weekly Banner*, Oct. 18, 1878, Jan. 31, Feb. 2 and 6, 1901; *Texas State Gazetteer and Business Directory, 1884*, 712; *Texas State Gazetteer and Business Directory, 1890–1891*, 1029; Schmidt, *Washington County*, 29; Grusendorf, "Education in Washington County," 169, 267, 270, 389–394, 418–419; Berger and Wilborn, "Education."

147. *Dallas Morning News*, May 11, 1902; *Texas State Gazetteer and Business Directory, 1884*, 712; *Texas State Gazetteer and Business Directory, 1890–1891*, 1029; Morris Card Files; "Record Book of Trustees for M.E. Church South at Washington"; Grusendorf, "Education in Washington County," 273; "St. Paul's Church, Navasota"; Betty Dunn, "The Reverends Ruter, Wesson, & Spencer in Navasota Oakland Cemetery," <http://www.texascenterforregionalstudies.com/the-reverends-ruter-wesson--spencer-in-navasota-oakland-cemetery.html> [Accessed Mar. 12, 2015]; Ernest A. Smith, *Martin Ruter* (Cincinnati, Ohio: Methodist Book Concern, 1915), 127; Cody, "Ruter," 33–34 (quotation); Phelan, *Early Methodism*, 428–429; Christian, "Washington-on-the-Brazos."

148. William R. Lott, "Washington Presbyterian Church," (manuscript), Apr. 10, 1891 (quotations; Star of the Republic Museum); Morris Card Files; Compiled Service Records for Texas Confederate Soldiers, 5th Texas Infantry: Jesse B. Lott and William R. Lott; *Official Register of the United States, 1885*, 2 vols. (Washington, D.C.: Government Printing Office, 1885), II, 651; Wheat, "Postmasters & Post Offices of Texas, 1846–1930: Washington County"; "Find a Grave: Robert A. Lott"; "Find a Grave: Jesse Bertram Lott," <http://www.findagrave.com/cgi-bin/fg.cgi?page=gr&GRid=52096197> [Accessed Mar. 16, 2015]; Gloria J. Manna, "Genealogy Report: Descendants of John Lott, Sr.," <http://familytreemaker.genealogy.com/users/m/a/n/Gloria-J-Manna/GENE12-0016.html> [Accessed Mar. 16, 2015]; Brown, *Indian Wars and Pioneers of Texas*, 431.

149. Moss, "Historical Summary," 17–18 (1st quotation); *Brenham Weekly Banner*, July 1, Aug. 5, 1897; *Dallas Morning News*, June 13, 1899 (3rd quotation); *Daily Statesman* (Austin), Nov. 26, 1899 (2nd quotation); *Brenham Daily Banner-Press*, Mar. 2, 1914 (4th–6th quotations); Pennington, *Washington County*, 14, 99, 105, 106 (7th and 8th quotations); Wheat, "Postmasters & Post Offices of Texas, 1846–1930: Washington County."

150. *Fort Worth Star-Telegram*, Sept. 25, 1906 (quotation); Nannie Hope to Mrs. C. A. Murphy, July 22, 1883 (Star of the Republic Museum); United States Thirteenth Census (1910), Washington County, Texas, Justice Precinct Number 1, 94th Enumeration District, Schedule 1 (Population), Record Group 29 (National Archives); Terry G. Jordan, "The German Settlement of Texas After 1865," *SHQ* 73 (October 1969): 198–199.

151. *Dallas Morning News*, Nov. 29, 1912, Jan. 11, 1955; *Fort Worth Star-Telegram*, Nov. 29, 1912; *Houston Post*, Nov. 29, 1912; *Bryan* (Tex.) *Daily Eagle and Pilot*, Jan. 9, 1913; *Brenham Daily Banner-Press*, June 4, Oct. 6, Nov. 17, 1914; Christian, "Washington-on-the-Brazos."

152. *Brenham Weekly Banner*, Jan. 3, 1907; *Brenham Daily Banner-Press*, Oct. 6, Nov. 17, 1914; *San Antonio Express*, Aug. 8 and 10, 1918; *Dallas Morning News*, July 24, Aug. 7, 1918; United States Fourteenth Census (1920), Washington County, Texas: Louis Kohlfarber, Schedule 1 (Population), Record Group 29 (National Archives); Wheat, "Postmasters & Post Offices of Texas, 1846–1930: Washington County."

153. United States Fourteenth Census (1920), Washington County, Texas: Precinct 1, Washington Village, Washington Voting Box, January 2, 3, 17, Schedule 1 (Population), Record Group 29 (National Archives); Wheat, "Postmasters & Post Offices of Texas, 1846–1930: Washington County."

154. *Brenham Daily Banner-Press*, Mar. 27 and 30, Apr. 17 and 22, June 16, Oct. 17, 1914, Apr. 17, 1917, May 18, 1918, Mar. 19, Sept. 23, 1919, Dec. 12, 1921, Mar. 1, 1922, Mar. 6, 1923; Grusendorf, "Education in Washington County," 418–420, 422–424; Schmidt, *Washington County*, 20; *110th Anniversary: History of Friedens Church of Washington, UCC, Washington, Texas* (n.p., [2000]), 11–13.

155. *Brenham Banner-Press*, Mar. 2, 1936; "Frieden's Church of Washington, United Church of Christ," <http://www.friedenschurch.com/aboutus.html> [Accessed Mar. 17, 2015]; Christian, "Washington-on-the-Brazos"; Oscar Mauzy, "Gilmer-Aikin Laws," *The Handbook of Texas Online*, <http://www.tshaonline.org/handbook/online/articles/mlg01> [Accessed March 17, 2015]. A plaque placed by the Works Progress Administration on the Old Washington school building declares that renovations were done from 1938 to 1940.

156. *Dallas Morning News*, Sept. 18, 1921 (1st quotation), Jan. 25, 1925, Mar. 3, 1929; United States Fourteenth Census (1920), Washington County, Texas: Precinct 1 (enumerated May 1, 1940), Schedule 1 (Population), Record Group 29 (National Archives); *The WPA Guide to Texas* (New York, 1940; reprint, Austin: Texas Monthly Press, 1986), 644 (2nd quotation).

157. *Dallas Morning News*, Feb. 2, 1947; Mark Friedberger, "'Mink and Manure': Rural Gentrification and Cattle Raising in Southeast Texas, 1945–1992," *SHQ* 102 (January 1999): 271–273, 275–279 (quotation), 282, 285–287, 291–292.

158. *Dallas Morning News*, July 26, 1960 (1st quotation), July 2, 1966 (2nd quotation); R. Henderson Shuffler, "Washington-on-the-Brazos: Texas' Birthplace," *Texas Parade* (March 1965), n.p. (3rd quotation); Mitch Green, "The Way We Weren't," *Texas Monthly* 3 (April 1975), 40, 44.

159. "Frieden's Church of Washington"; "Blessed Virgin Mary Catholic Church, Washington, TX," <http://home.catholicweb.com/Blessed_Virgin_Mary_Catholic_Church/> [Accessed Mar. 17, 2015]; "Barbecue Time Machine: Washington Sons of Hermann," <http://zenbbq.com/2011/10/barbecue-time-machine/> [Accessed Mar. 17, 2015]; Clyde McQueen, *Black Churches in Texas: A Guide to Historic Congregations* (College Station: Texas A&M University Press, 2000), 72–80; David A. Williams (ed.), *Bricks Without Straw: A Comprehensive History of African Americans in Texas* (Austin: Eakin Press, 1997), 314–315.

Chapter 6: STATE HISTORIC SITE

160. Gregg Cantrell, "The Bones of Stephen F. Austin: History and Memory in Progressive-Era Texas," *Lone Star Pasts: History and Memory in Texas*, ed. Elizabeth H. Turner and Gregg Cantrell (College Station: Texas A&M University Press, 2006), 39–73; Pennington, *Washington County*, 106 (quotation).

161. *Brenham Weekly Banner*, July 3 (1st and 2nd quotations), Oct. 9 (3rd quotation), 1890, July 9, 1891, July 8, 1897; "Find a Grave: Walter Nathaniel Norwood"; Anne W. Hooker, "Buchanan, James Paul," *The Handbook of Texas Online*, <http://www.tshaonline.org/handbook/online/articles/fbuo1> [Accessed Mar. 11, 2015].

162. *Dallas Morning News*, June 18, 1899, Mar. 1, 1923, Mar. 3, 1929; *Daily Statesman* (Austin), Nov. 26, 1899; *Houston Post*, Feb. 13, Apr. 22, 1900 (quotation); Pennington, *Washington County*, 97; James L. Hailey, "Bryan, Beauregard," *The Handbok of Texas Online*, <http://www. tshaonline.org/handbook/online/articles/fbrak> [Accessed Mar. 11, 2015]; J. A. Reynolds, "Burleson, Rufus Columbus," *The Handbook of Texas Online*, <http://www.tshaonline.org/handbook/online/articles/fbu44> [Accessed Mar. 11, 2015]; Irby C. Nichols Jr., "Terrell, Alexander Watkins," *The Handbook of Texas Online*, <http://www.tshaonline.org/handbook/online/articles/fte16> [Accessed Mar. 11, 2015].

163. *Dallas Morning News*, Dec. 8, 1902; *Brenham Daily Banner-Press*, Feb. 7, Apr. 15 and 23, May 6, 7, and 16, Aug. 28, Sept. 4, 1914, Mar. 2, May 21 and 29, Dec. 10, 1915; Pennington, *Washington County*, 97–98; H. Roger Grant, "Interurbans are the Wave of the Future," *SHQ* 84 (July 1980): 35–36; Ledbetter, "Fisher, Orceneth."

164. *Brenham Daily Banner-Press*, Apr. 22, Aug. 17, 20, 22, and 27, Sept. 5, Oct. 9, 1914; *Dallas Morning News*, Aug. 17, 1914; Wheat, "Postmasters & Post Offices of Texas, 1846–1930: Washington County"; "Find a Grave: Gustav Stolz (1872–1914)," <http://www.findagrave.com/cgi-bin/fg.cgi?page=gr&GRid=70995432> [Accessed Mar. 11, 2015].

165. *Brenham Daily Banner-Press*, Oct. 7 and 9, Dec. 17, 1914, Jan. 8, Mar. 24, Apr. 5, 1915, May 28, 1918; *Dallas Morning News*, Mar. 30, Sept. 25, 1926; Wheat, "Postmasters & Post Offices of Texas, 1846–1930: Washington County"; "Find a Grave: Gustav Stolz (1872–1914)"; "Find a Grave: Gustav Stolz, Jr.," <http://www.findagrave.com/cgi-bin/fg.cgi?page=gr&GSsr=561&GScid=2161491&GRid=70995394&> [Accessed Mar. 11, 2015].

166. *Brenham Daily Banner-Press*, Feb. 20, Mar. 22, May 21, 1915; *Heraldo de Brownsville*, May 8, 1939; *Dallas Morning News*, Mar. 1, 1923, May 8, 1939; H. P. N. Gammel (comp.), *The Laws of Texas: Supplement Volume to the Original Ten Volumes*, Vol. 17: 1915–1917 (Austin: Gammel's Book Store, 1917), 641–642; Pennington, *Washington County*, 94–98.

167. *Fort Worth Star-Telegram*, Dec. 21, 1915; *Brenham Daily Banner-Press*, Mar. 1, 2, and 3, 1916; *Dallas Morning News*, Mar. 3, 1916.

168. *Brenham Daily Banner-Press*, Mar. 6, Sept. 1, 1916, Jan. 25, 1918, Jan. 10, 1919; *Houston Chronicle*, June 13, 1917; *Dallas Morning News*, Sept. 18, 1921; "Speech of Stella Martin Brosig," (manuscript), n.d. (quotation), (Star of the Republic Museum); *Supplemental Biennial Report of the Secretary of State, 1918* (Austin: A. C. Baldwin & Sons, 1918), 23; H. P. N. Gammel (comp.), *The Laws of Texas: Supplement Volume to the Original Ten Volumes*, Vol. 18: 1917–1918 (Austin: Gammel's Book Store, 1918), 847; "Washington on the Brazos State Park Conceptual Study" (typescript), June 1972, Texas Parks and Wildlife Department Records,

State Parks Division, Box 2004/090-10 (TSLA); Texas Secretary of State, Statutory Documents, Deeds File: Washington on the Brazos Park, Box 2-10/294 (TSLA).

169. *Brenham Daily Banner-Press*, Dec. 12, 1921; *Dallas Morning News*, Dec. 30, 1921; "Brosig Speech"; Bluefford Hancock and William C. Welch, "The 'British Connection': Brenham and Texas' Early Nurserymen," *Aggie Horticulture*, <http://aggie-horticulture.tamu.edu/newsletters/hortupdate/2010/jul_aug/britconn.html> [Accessed Mar. 11, 2015]; H. P. N. Gammel (comp.), *The Laws of Texas: Supplement Volume to the Original Ten Volumes, Vol. 19: 1919* (Austin: Gammel's Book Store, 1919), 1243; H. P. N. Gammel (comp.), *The Laws of Texas: Supplement Volume to the Original Ten Volumes, Vol. 21: 1921* (Austin: Gammel's Book Store, 1921) 180, 739–40; "Washington on the Brazos State Park Conceptual Study."

170. *Dallas Morning News*, Sept. 18, 1921, Jan. 25, Mar. 15, 1925, May 5, 1926, Feb. 27, Mar. 12, 1957; *Brenham Daily Banner-Press*, Jan. 10, 1919 (quotation), Mar. 1, 1923; "Brosig Speech"; Shuffler, "Signing," 332; Schmidt, *Washington County*, 45; Texas State Board of Control, Records: Members, Box 1991/016-35: Washington State Park, 1924–1928 (TSLA); Texas State Board of Control: Records: Washington on the Brazos Contracts, Boxes 1991/016-96 and 1991/016-111 (TSLA); Miguel A. L. Trujillo, "Lights and Shadows in Texas Preservation: The Case of Washington-on-the-Brazos State Park," <http://www2.uah.es/histant/ trujillo/ wob/ wob.htm#N_9_> [Accessed Mar. 11, 2015]; "Page Southerland Page, LLP of Austin," <http://www. thc.state.tx.us/page-southerland-page-llp-austin> [Accessed May 21, 2015].

171. *Houston Post*, Apr. 28, 1936; *Dallas Morning News*, June 29, 1936, Feb. 21, Mar. 7, 1937, Feb. 27, 1938; *Houston Chronicle*, "Texas Magazine," Feb. 15, 1970; Texas State Board of Control, Records: Washington on the Brazos Contracts, Box 1991/016-112 (TSLA); H. P. N. Gammel (comp.), *The Laws of Texas: Supplement Volume to the Original Ten Volumes, Vol. 25: 1927* (Austin: Gammel's Book Store, 1927), 870; H. P. N. Gammel (comp.), *The Laws of Texas: Supplement Volume to the Original Ten Volumes, Vol. 26: 1929* (Austin: Gammel's Book Store, 1929), 1561; H. P. N. Gammel (comp.), *The Laws of Texas: Supplement Volume to the Original Ten Volumes, Vol. 29: 1934–1935* (Austin: Gammel's Book Store, 1935), 1144; H. P. N. Gammel (comp.), *The Laws of Texas: Supplement Volume to the Original Ten Volumes, Vol. 30: 1935–1937* (Austin: Gammel's Book Store, 1937), 2166; Dietrich, *Blazing Story*, 102, 105; Trujillo, "Lights and Shadows"; "Washington on the Brazos State Park Conceptual Study."

172. *Dallas Morning News*, Feb. 16 and 21, Mar. 1 and 3, 1936, Feb. 21, 1937, Feb. 27, 1938; Vertical File: Washington-on-the-Brazos (CAH).

173. *Dallas Morning News*, Feb. 21, 1937, Feb. 27, Mar. 1 and 3, 1938, Mar. 26,1940, Mar. 3, 1941, Mar. 2 and 3, 1942, Mar. 2, 1944; *Brenham Banner-Press*, Feb. 10, 1940; Vertical File: Washington-on-the-Brazos (CAH).

174. *Dallas Morning News*, Dec. 11, 1937, Feb. 26, Mar. 1, 2, 3, and 5, May 8, 1939, Feb. 24, Mar. 3, 1949; *Heraldo de Brownsville*, Mar. 2 and 3, May 8, 1939; H. P. N. Gammel (comp.), *The Laws of Texas: Supplement Volume to the Original Ten Volumes, Vol. 31: 1937–1939* (Austin: Gammel's Book Store, 1939), 1098–1099; McLean, *Robertson's Colony*, XIII, 146–153, 158–160; Vertical File: Washington-on-the-Brazos (CAH); Dietrich, *Blazing Story*, 107; Ericson, "Childress, George Campbell"; Christopher Long, "Nelson, Donald Siegfried," *The Handbook of Texas Online*, <http://www.tshaonline.org/handbook/online/articles/fnejz> [Accessed Mar. 11, 2015].

175. *Dallas Morning News*, June 19 and 28, 1946, Jan. 21, 1953; "Washington

on the Brazos State Park Conceptual Study"; H. Bailey Carroll, "Texas Collection," *SHQ* 59 (October 1955): 227–228; H. Bailey Carroll, "Texas Collection," *SHQ* 59 (April 1956): 507–508; Siegel, *Big Men Walked Here*, 98–99; Daniel Murph, "Daniel, Marion Price, Sr.," *The Handbook of Texas Online*, <http://www.tshaonline.org/handbook/online/articles/fda94> [Accessed Mar. 11, 2015]; D. Ryan Smith, "Star Of The Republic Museum," *The Handbook of Texas Online*, <http://www.tshaonline.org/handbook/online/articles/lbs04> [Accessed Mar. 11, 2015]; Christopher Long, "Washington-on-the-Brazos State Historic Site," *The Handbook of Texas Online*, <http://www.tshaonline.org/handbook/online/articles/gkw02)> [Accessed Mar. 11, 2015].

176. *Dallas Morning News*, Dec. 4, 1955, Feb. 15, Apr. 15, 1956, Nov. 26, 1958, July 26, 1960; *Houston Post*, Dec. 25, 1955; *Austin Statesman*, Sept. 7, 1955, Feb. 17, 1956; *Austin American*, Feb. 17, 1956; Minutes of the City Council, City of Austin, Texas, Nov. 2, 1961, <http://www.austintexas.gov/edims/document.cfm?id=41163> [Accessed May 21, 2015]; Siegel, *Big Men Walked Here*, 98.

177. *Brenham Banner-Press*, Mar. 3, 1959, Mar. 3, 1960, Mar. 1, 1961; *Houston Chronicle*, Feb. 22 and 28, Mar. 3, 1963; Shuffler, "Signing," 313.

178. *Dallas Morning News*, Sept. 8 and 27, 1966, Mar. 12, 1967, Feb. 24 and 28, 1970; *Houston Chronicle*, "Texas Magazine," Feb. 15, 1970; *Brenham Banner-Press*, Feb. 27, 1970; "Washington on the Brazos State Park Conceptual Study"; Friedberger, "Mink and Manure," 277; Joe B. Frantz, "Texas Collection, *SHQ* 70 (April 1967): 647–648; Green, "The Way We Weren't," 40; Siegel, *Big Men Walked Here*, 98–100; Betty Plummer, *Historic Homes of Washington County, 1821–1860* (San Marcos, Tex.: Rio Fresco Books, 1971), 11–20, 37–44; Smith, "Star Of The Republic Museum"; Lel Purcell Hawkins, "Red, George Clark," *The Handbook of Texas Online*, <http://www.tshaonline.org/handbook/online/articles/fre07> [Accessed Mar. 11, 2015].

179. *Dallas Morning News*, Mar. 12, 1967, Mar. 1, June 2, 1968, Feb. 28, 1970; *Houston Chronicle*, "Texas Magazine," Feb. 15, 1970; Friedberger, "Mink and Manure," 277; Mott and Corbin, *Archeological Investigations*, 1; Rhiana D. Casias, "From Prehistoric to Counter-Culture: An Archaeological Survey of Peaceable Kingdom Farm, Washington County, Texas" (M.A. thesis, Texas Tech University, 2013), 40, 49–50; Trujillo, "Lights and Shadows."

180. *Houston Chronicle*, "Texas Magazine," Feb. 15, 1970; *Dallas Morning News*, Feb. 28, 1970; *San Antonio Express-News*, Feb. 26, 1977; Siegel, *Big Men Walked Here*, 100; Gammel, *Laws of Texas: Supplement*, XXX, 624; Trujillo, "Lights and Shadows"; Kendall Curlee, "Normann, Charles Berkeley," *The Handbook of Texas Online*, <http://www.tshaonline.org/handbook/online/articles/fno18> [Accessed Mar. 11, 2015].

181. *Houston Post*, Dec. 25, 1955; *Dallas Morning News*, June 2, 1968, Feb. 28, 1970; *Brenham Banner-Press*, Feb. 27, 1970; Siegel, *Big Men Walked Here*, 98–100, 103; "Washington on the Brazos State Park Conceptual Study Trujillo, "Lights and Shadows"; Diana J. Kleiner, "Bybee, Charles L.," *The Handbook of Texas Online*, <http://www.tshaonline.org/handbook/online/articles/fby08> [Accessed Mar. 11, 2015].

182. *Houston Chronicle*, "Texas Magazine," Feb. 15, 1970; *Dallas Morning News*, Feb. 24 and 28, Mar. 2, 1970; *Brenham Banner-Press*, Feb. 27, 1970; "Washington on the Brazos State Park Conceptual Study"; McLean, *Robertson's Colony*, XIII, 158–170; Smith, "Star of the Republic Museum."

183. *Brenham Banner-Press*, Feb. 27, 1970; *Dallas Morning News*, May 13,

1971, Mar. 7, 1973; John G. Johnson, "Dirty Thirty," *The Handbook of Texas Online*, <http://www.tshaonline.org/handbook/online/articles/wmdsh> [Accessed Mar. 11, 2015].

184. *Houston Chronicle*, "Texas Magazine," Feb. 15, 1970; *Dallas Morning News*, Feb. 27, 1976; *Houston Chronicle*, Feb. 27, 1977; Green, "The Way We Weren't," 40–42, 44; Mott and Corbin, *Archaeological Investigations*, 3; Smith, "Star of the Republic Museum"; Long, "Washington-on-the-Brazos State Historic Site."

185. *Dallas Morning News*, Feb. 28, 1970, Dec. 19, 1975, Aug. 7, 1983; *Houston Chronicle*, "Texas Magazine," Feb. 15, 1970; Mary Love-Bigony, "A Texas Star is Reborn," *Texas Highways* 56 (March 1998), 21–22 (quotation); "Southwestern Collection," *SHQ* 99 (January 1996): 406; Smith, "Star of the Republic Museum"; Trujillo, "Lights and Shadows."

186. *Dallas Morning News*, July 2, 1966; Love-Bigony, "Texas Star is Reborn," 22; McLean, *Robertson's Colony*, XIII, 158–170; "Texas History Page: Washington Lodge No. 18, A.F. & A.M.," <http://texashistorypage.com/Washington-Lodge-No.-18-Washington-on-the-Brazos.html> [Accessed Mar. 11, 2015].

INDEX